Nigel Marsh is the bestselling author of *Fat, Forty and Fired*, *Overworked and Underlaid* and *Fit, Fifty and Fired Up*. He is the co-founder of Earth Hour, the founder of the Sydney Skinny, the host of the award-winning podcast The Five of My Life, and a proud ambassador of the Australian Indigenous Education Foundation. He also came second last in the 2005 Bondi-to-Bronte ocean race.

Highly in demand as a public speaker, Nigel regularly gives speeches to major corporations on both his business and personal views. His TED speech on work-life balance remains one of the most viewed outside of America.

Smart, Stupid & Sixty

Nigel Marsh

WILLIAM HEINEMANN: AUSTRALIA

WILLIAM HEINEMANN

UK | USA | Canada | Ireland | Australia
India | New Zealand | South Africa | China

William Heinemann is part of the Penguin Random House group of companies
whose addresses can be found at global.penguinrandomhouse.com

Penguin
Random House
Australia

First published by William Heinemann in 2022
Copyright © Nigel Marsh 2022

Cover image by Kerrick/iStock
Cover design by Adam Laszczuk © Penguin Random House Australia Pty Ltd
Typeset in 13/16.5 pt Adobe Garamond Pro by Midland Typesetters, Australia

Printed and bound in Australia by Griffin Press, part of Ovato, an accredited
ISO AS/NZS 14001 Environmental Management Systems printer

A catalogue record for this
book is available from the
NATIONAL LIBRARY OF AUSTRALIA National Library of Australia

ISBN 978 0 14379 436 3

penguin.com.au

We at Penguin Random House Australia acknowledge that Aboriginal and Torres Strait
Islander peoples are the Traditional Custodians and the first storytellers of the lands on which we
live and work. We honour Aboriginal and Torres Strait Islander peoples' continuous connection
to Country, waters, skies and communities. We celebrate Aboriginal and Torres Strait Islander
stories, traditions and living cultures; and we pay our respects to Elders past and present.

For
Eve, Grace, Harry, Alex

Prologue

FOR AS LONG as I can remember my mother answered her telephone in exactly the same way. Not by saying 'hello'. Not by stating her name. Nor by enquiring who was calling.

No. My dear mum answered the phone by saying, 'Marston Magna 850172.'

Always.

As I write this I can clearly hear the business-like tone in which she said it. Somehow putting energy and meaning into the numbers and ending with a friendly little uplift on her delivery of the '2'.

It's a generational thing. Like many people in their eighties, Mum spent her early childhood hearing her parents do it, as back then it was a useful way of letting the caller know if they'd been put through to the correct number by the telephonist at a small rural community's manual switchboard.

However, it was now a behaviour whose original purpose had long passed, and was retained solely out of habit.

Over the years I tried to get Mum to stop telling me her phone number when I called.

'Marston Magna . . .' she'd start.

'Mum, it's me . . .' I'd interject.

'850 . . .' she'd bulldoze on.

'Nigel . . .' I'd try again.

'172,' she'd finish.

'Mum, you know you needn't recite your number when you pick up the phone,' I'd venture gently.

'Don't be silly, Nidgey,' she said, using one of her favourite nicknames for me. (Strangely, she always pronounced it to rhyme with 'midge'. But hey, it was preferable to 'Birdy Face', one of her other favourites.) 'If I don't, how will people know if they've got through to the right person?'

'They'd find out soon enough when they speak to you. But forget other people – when it's *me* calling, I know it's you. You're my mum.'

'Mmmm . . .' she'd say non-committally, employing her version of the consent and evade strategy at which she was an Olympic champion.

And she'd then carry on exactly as before. I'd drop it because, let's face it, there are other more important things in life to worry about. Recently, however, I started my campaign again as I had taken to calling her every day.

Mum's health had taken a worrying turn for the worse. She was already struggling with myeloma and the effects of chemotherapy, but now she was also increasingly out of breath and had been rushed to hospital on two occasions as her lungs were filling up with liquid – giving her the appalling sensation of drowning from within. After her last visit, she had been diagnosed with inoperable Stage 4 lung cancer. The 'cancer motherload' so to speak, or as Mum put it, 'I've got a two-for-one deal, Nidgey.'

I was urgently making arrangements to come over to see her as it looked increasingly likely that there mightn't be the opportunity for many more trips in the future. In the meantime, she insisted on painstakingly starting each of our conversations by pointlessly telling me her phone number.

I decided to try a new tactic.

'Marston Magna 850172,' she said upon answering the phone, when I next called.

'Oh sorry, I wanted Marston Magna 85017 . . . 3,' I replied, before hanging up.

To her credit she was still laughing when I rang back. But did it stop her telling me her phone number from then on? Did it hell – they don't make them like my mum anymore.

Introduction

I HAVE WRITTEN three books before this. To my surprise and delight, the first one, *Fat, Forty and Fired*, was a bestseller locally and even enjoyed a modicum of success internationally. It was translated into a number of languages and the film and TV rights were bought and trips to Hollywood enjoyed. To this day it is what they call in the trade 'a good backlister', still stocked and sold in shops twenty years later.

As the title suggests, *Fat, Forty and Fired* describes the year I lost my job – as an overweight forty-year-old. Long story short: having fallen off the corporate hamster wheel, I decided I needed to stay off it. Easier said than done with no income and four young kids to provide for.

But despite the risk and uncertainty, I was *convinced* I had to reassess and reprioritise my life. After serious reflection I resolved to try to change my life in every way. I wanted to put the people I loved, and the things I valued, at the centre of my life, not leave them at the edges – as my career had been forcing me to – ever again. And that required having to face the very real fear, and inevitable downsides, involved in genuine change and refusing to do things simply because they're the conventional path.

It's a constant challenge but I'm every bit as committed to my resolution now as I was twenty years ago. In some ways you could say this book is a once a decade check-in to hold myself to account – to see if I'm still on the right track as I head into my seventh decade, with all the new issues that involves.

I've had two books published since *Fat, Forty and Fired,* one of which was my first check-in, *Fit, Fifty and Fired Up.* Whilst dear to my heart and mildly successful locally, they didn't attract any international attention and sank with barely a trace after the natural short lifespan of a book these days. My writing career could be said to be going in reverse. Initial success followed by gentle decline.

Despite this, over the years since my first book came out I have repeatedly been asked when my next one is going to be published. I'm never quite sure if this is because people would welcome it or want reassurance I've given up flogging a dead horse. Irrespective, my stock answer for a number of years was: 'When I'm fifty'. Which turned out to be true (exhibit A: *Fit, Fifty and Fired Up*). And in more recent times, since my half-century it has been: 'When I'm sixty'.

On the one hand it was a useful way of dodging the question, but on the other it contained an element of truth. I have come to like the idea of writing a book once a decade.

It is often said that 'the unexamined life isn't worth living'. Wise words, but at the same time it could equally valuably be said that 'the overexamined life is rarely worth reading about'.

With the glorious exceptions of geniuses like Stephen Fry or Bill Bryson – who seem to be able to crank out classics twice a year whilst standing on their heads – it is an unfortunate reality of the modern world that there are far too many new books. I'm reluctant to add to this mountain.

I have one friend who decided on his sixtieth birthday to only read books that were more than fifty years old. It's been four years and he's happily sticking to the plan. You would have to live a number of lifetimes to be able to read all of the good books published in the nineteenth and twentieth centuries alone. The world doesn't *need* any more books. And I don't feel I have the right, or indeed the will, to write a new one every year either. Conversely, however, I am hugely excited to do so every ten.

Things happen in a decade that bear examining – some painful and sad, like the passing of parents or the increasing destruction of the planet; some funny and joyous, like having adult kids, or working with young people, others thought-provoking and challenging, like ageing and your own impending death.

My views have changed on a number of issues. And I view that as a positive. I have changed my mind before and I will again. Re-reading my previous books, I've quite frankly felt embarrassed on a number of occasions. But, hey, if you're not frequently embarrassed by yourself, I reckon you're not trying hard enough – or you're in danger of taking yourself way too seriously. One of my favourite writers, Alain de Botton, maintains that 'if we are not regularly deeply embarrassed by who we are, the journey to self-knowledge hasn't begun'.

Probably when I re-read *this* book in years to come, I'll also be embarrassed. And that's fine. So here it is – my next 'decade' book. Looking back over my fifties and forward to my sixties. I don't expect foreign translations and film deals (although I wouldn't complain), but I do hope my regular readers enjoy and get something of value from what follows. If you don't, I apologise in advance for the fact that I have every intention of writing another one when I get to seventy.

If I get to seventy.

1

Smart, stupid and sixty

I WAS RECENTLY moaning to Kate that I couldn't remember where I'd put the car keys and muttered, in a jokey resigned way, 'Must be early-onset dementia.' My twenty-two-year-old daughter Eve overheard, raised an eyebrow and simply said, 'Early?' Nice.

The week before, Harry's twenty-four-year-old girlfriend, Lea, had asked me, 'Nigel, who's the nice old man who puts the lane ropes in at Swim Club?' It turns out she was referring to my friend Bob – who is younger than me. Ouch.

Let's be honest, though, despite all the wonderful advances in medicine and science you don't see many 120-year-olds walking around. Sixty is not *middle* aged. It's old. And there is nothing wrong with that. Better to own it than deny it.

I don't want to encourage a sad delusional denial of the ageing process. We need to reclaim the word 'old'. It shouldn't be a pejorative term when we use it to describe people; after all, it isn't when we use it to describe things. More often than not, 'old' to describe a church or work of art has positive connotations. Of beauty, quality, having stood the test of time etc. A similar status should be reclaimed for old human beings. The American writer Anne Lamott coined a wonderful phrase, 'We contain all the ages we have ever been.' With that perspective, when she looks at a sixty-year-old she *includes* her fifty, forty, thirty, twenty-year-old selves. How fantastic is that?

However, the society we live in makes it hard to gain that knowledge – as it gives out the powerful signal, which is reinforced everywhere, that older people are worth less than younger people. And that your old age will be nothing but a sad period of abject misery and decline.

With all that in mind, as I embarked on this book, I needed to settle on a title. I was keen for a similar one to my 'forty' and 'fifty' books, but as the ideas rolled in – *Sad, Sixty and Senile*, my original thought; or my wife Kate's suggestion, *Celebrating, Sixty and Saggy*; or even my brother's helpful contribution, *Smug, Supercilious and Self-Satisfied* – none seemed to really capture what I was hoping to communicate in the book.

In the end, I decided on *Smart, Stupid and Sixty*. We can debate the percentages that should be applied to the first two words, but overall I'm happy that it's an accurate, honest and not-too-up-itself description.

I also like the contradictory feel of 'Smart' and 'Stupid'. I'm not all one or the other – which is a theme relevant to being sixty. Because whilst your seventh decade brings with it a whole host of inevitabilities, not all of them are bad.

The unavoidable reality is there is good stuff and bad stuff about *every* life stage (just ask any masturbating teenager who can't get laid).

We might not have a choice about many of the bad things – but we've got a choice about how we deal with them. At the risk of painting a dark picture, I want to be able to face a shrinking career, shrinking family, shrinking finances, shrinking health – and ever closer death – and *still have a blast.*

A few years ago I was honoured to be asked to give the speech at my son's school's Year 12 graduation dinner. I agonised long and hard about how to send the right mix of messages to these young men. I was nervous about baring my soul and making a fool of myself in front of the parent and teacher group (many of whom I socialised with), but decided that honesty was the best policy.

Taking a deep breath, I opened with, 'Gentlemen, life is either a daring adventure or it is nothing at all. Your objective as you leave this place tonight shouldn't be to tiptoe gently through your life, so you arrive safely at your grave with a well-preserved body. The objective should be to slide in sideways completely exhausted, yelling, "Holy crap, that was fantastic!" It doesn't matter how you go in this life, as long as you at least *have* a go.'

I meant it then for them, with their whole lives spread out before them, but I realise that it equally applies to me now. If there were such a thing as a graduation dinner for the parents as they turned sixty – and if again I had to make a speech – I'd open with the same quote with the smallest of amendments. I'd say that 'old age' – rather than 'life' – is a daring adventure. The rest, I believe, applies every bit as powerfully.

2

Rice field rabbit

I'M REPEATEDLY WARNED that kids growing up and leaving home is a massive blow that leaves a huge hole in your life. That after the twenty years painstakingly spent trying to develop the skills of being a good parent, the moment you feel you've got close to fitting the description that role might seem to be obsolete.

But I disagree. The role is still needed, it just changes. You still play a valuable role. Even if it is only in the background.

My friend Ruth tells a story about the time she visited her elderly parents and as she walked up the driveway she could hear her dad shouting from the back garden to her mum in the sitting room, 'Darling, when are we expecting the kids?' Fabulous – 'the kids'. All three of whom were over sixty. Because truth is they *never* stop being your kids.

Despite the decreasing amounts of time in each other's physical presence, I want my kids to have an unshakeable hard-wired belief that whatever else is uncertain in this world they can rely 100 per cent on my unconditional love for as long as I draw breath. And that, if I can pull it off, is as valuable a role as any other. For them to have someone they know they can rely on, come what may, as they make their own way in the world.

Other people have told me the fun times leave the home when the kids do. I haven't found this to be true either. The fun doesn't stop, it just changes. Being taken to see comedians you've never heard of, welcoming new partners to the family home, listening to horror stories of first jobs, even on occasion, Praise The Lord, having dinner cooked for you. The list of new memories being created to add to the old cherished 'bedtime stories' ones is endless.

A surprising source of a number of those new memories is social media. I say surprising not just because social media is well known to be generally corrosive to any genuine human connection, but also because I'm a laggard when it comes to using it.

I do so because I have to for my various roles, but it's not something I naturally can get excited about – having always viewed it as a vast digital open sewer winding its way around the globe full of the worst examples of the human mind, juxtaposed with cute images of puppies above hackneyed inspirational quotes.

And all expressed in moronic language. 'The internet breaks over Meghan's new haircut' and 'Ronaldo's new shorts melt the Web' are a couple of examples from a quick glance at my feed this morning. 'breaks', 'loses it', 'shattered', 'shut down', 'melts'. Yet five minutes after these utterly trivial stories were posted, the internet was of course being 'shattered' and 'broken' again by something equally trivial. And five minutes later, it was being blasted to smithereens by someone else's new haircut. If these clickbait headlines were even remotely accurate about the catastrophic consequences of ex-Royals' follicular preferences or what Portuguese footballers like to do with their shorts, the poor old internet would be in a billion pieces by lunchtime most days.

And the oversharing. Spare me the oversharing. 'I love this man more every day. For eight years he has been my rock, my inspiration, my lover and my best friend. Blessed to be sharing my life journey with you my sexy Prince. Happy anniversary xoxo!!'

Now imagine for a moment this couple actually does have a fabulous relationship. Wouldn't it be better to send this declaration of love solely to the Prince himself? Why are you sharing it with all of your 2317 Facebook friends? Have we asked you for updates on how blessed you feel in your love life, or are you just assuming we find you and your sexy Prince mesmerising? The truth is, I probably don't even know who this person is.

But the happiness bragging is nothing compared to the relentless virtue signalling. Because social media offers us the intoxicating bliss of moral grandstanding without accountability, you haven't got to achieve, or even do, anything – just post about it.

I often find myself in the bizarre situation where I can wholeheartedly agree with someone's stated climate-change (or whatever) point of view but simply can't stand their holier-than-thou posturing. The chest-beating finger-wagging almost makes me want to not recycle.

And it's so often just that – posturing. That person relentlessly sermonising about public education sent her two youngest kids to the most expensive school in New South Wales. That annoyingly shouty climate activist drives an SUV the size of a Sherman tank; or, with a breathtaking lack of self-awareness, brags about doing the Camino Trail that she took two greenhouse-gas-contributing long-haul flights to get to. It's so easy to be self-satisfyingly woke on Instagram – rather less easy, but considerably more impressive and inspirational, in real life.

And don't get me started on how people's own social-media echo chambers drive them into ever more deluded extremism. In the competition to prove they are more outraged than their followers – who by the way are also trying to win their own online arms race – they develop, spout and, worryingly, *believe* ever more ridiculous views.

Alongside the moronic posts about the world melting and the internet breaking, my quick scroll this morning revealed a post from someone claiming 'Scott Morrison is as bad as Hitler'. Really? The democratically elected former prime minister of Australia is as bad as that German geezer who outlawed democratic elections in 1933 and spent the next decade murderously trying to establish a hate-fuelled thousand-year Reich? Umm . . . try selling that line to the descendants of families who fled the Holocaust to start a new life in Australia.

It's hard to know where to start in the face of such idiocy. I try to be charitable, imagining that what this person actually means is: 'I think Scott Morrison is a bit of a dill, a marketing-driven visionless lightweight, and I *hated* his immigration policy – I'm glad he was voted out of power.' But if they mean that, why don't they *say* it? Because unfortunately social media has turned their brains to custard, that's why, and 'recreational outrage' is now a thing.

I was so fascinated by this particular Hitler post that I looked at the rest of the online footprint of the person who posted it. By all accounts she appears to be a lovely and loving member of her family and community. *Which makes it all the more terrifying.* If this is what social media can do to a 'normal' person, I shudder to think of the effect it has on the already extreme, frothing at the mouth, swivel-eyed loons who definitely don't need any encouragement.

And yet . . . and yet . . . there are also so many wonderful aspects about social media. As I approach sixty, one of my greatest loves has become Facebook Messenger. My daughter Eve set up a family group chat and it is a daily source of joy. It's like my own secret guilty pleasure – interacting with all my closest family at once.

It's almost the online version of those long car trips I used to love, as the whole family – wife, dog and all four kids – were trapped together for hours on our way to West Wyalong. Some of my most treasured memories are of the banter pinging around our cramped, battered Toyota Tarago, as inevitably one of the kids was travel sick not entirely successfully into the too-small bag hastily provided. Deep and intricate relationships were being formed that will last a lifetime. Truly the important stuff.

Well, I'm going out on a bendy limb here and suggesting Messenger is even better. For a start, it happens every day, it takes far less time than driving to West Wyalong and, best of all, there's no semi-digested chocolate to scrub out of the back-seat upholstery. It is also personally, uniquely *us*. The Marsh family.

I have no idea how it was set up, but I love the fact that it appears on my phone as 'Marshmellows'. And we all have nicknames: Chest (Noodolo) Dent, Rice Field Rabbit, 440 Not 420, Arnicate, Low Key Scar and I Left The Lonely Planet Book At La Veranda.

Just looking at that list makes me smile with love for each person concerned and the memory that created their particular name. Even if one of them is a drug reference, another Vietnamese slang for a rat and the longer one in honour of one of the most irritating things any human being has ever done on the first day of a family holiday. Gorgeous, all of them. And a welcome evolution on early family car nicknames like Phil McGroin and Dixie Normous.

I love it so much that I deliberately use it to send individual messages so all the family is in on every conversation. Again, replicating the 'long car-journey vibe'. Something as innocent and banal as 'Grace I can't believe you finished all the milk' can result in an extended multi-person conversation as children who are not even in the same country chip in with abuse and banter.

So that is probably the thing I am most grateful to Zuckerberg for. I can forgive him for the torrential stream of idiotic headlines, vacuous bikini selfies and moronically myopic political messaging, as long as I can feel close and engaged and connected to my family members, irrespective of our actual physical location.

3

The Five of My Life

AT SOME STAGE in my fifties I developed an increasing habit, when discussing good things, of always referencing related bad things. So, rather than saying, 'That was a great film last night,' I'd say, 'That was a great film last night, *unlike those other two rubbish ones we saw at the festival.*' I'd do it even when having no other intention than being complimentary.

On one such occasion Kate and I bumped into a man at the beach who played in a band made up of dads from the local school. I had seen him play at a friend's sixtieth the week before. It was fantastic and I decided to tell him so.

'That was such a great gig on Saturday, Tim. Loved it, just loved it. The band is amazing. Really surprisingly good. I've seen a lot of amateur bands and usually they're awful . . .'

And off I went describing how bad some of the other bands I'd seen had been. Later that night Kate pointed out that I'd done it yet again and asked me why. I genuinely don't know. In some ways it is a hamfisted attempt to be even nicer. I'm telling you how shite the others were as a way of emphasising how great you were.

Not such a big problem, I suppose, but I wasn't happy with it. Particularly as, left unchecked, it might have developed into a subconscious all-encompassing negative default setting. To this point, worryingly, Kate had remarked in recent years that I'd become increasingly judgemental of others. Unfortunately, she was right (she usually is). My conversational quirk of defining good things in contrast to related bad ones was morphing into an unattractive habit of seeing the negatives in people. Spotting their flaws, not the strengths, and, worse, remarking on them. Awful.

I'd listen to a relationship expert selling her new book of advice and muse, 'Well, you're divorced twice so it can't be that effective counsel,' or read a business guru describing the characteristics of great companies and not being able to help pointing out that all his examples have subsequently under-performed compared to their competition. Or watching some motivational fitness personality lecturing his clients on TV about how they have to commit to daily hard work in the gym if they're going to achieve their fitness goals and blurting out at him, 'Every day is gym day . . . when you're running away from yourself.'

Ironically, not only do I have no right to do this, being every bit as flawed as anyone else, I actually dearly want to see the best in people. I subscribe to the Quaker philosophy that there is a little bit of God in everyone. (If the 'G' word is too off-putting, add an extra 'o' in the middle and the philosophy works just as well.) I don't *want* to be unfairly or harshly judgemental, but the uncomfortable truth is that in my fifties that had become my subconscious default setting. I wasn't happy with that, so I decided to take serious action to correct this flaw before my sixties.

And that's where The Five of My Life comes in. A few years ago I decided I wanted to create an interview show that would be enjoyable, thought-provoking content, and at the same time help make me a better man – by, among many other things, forcing me on a regular basis to see, look for and discuss only the good in both things and people.

The concept was simple. I would interview 'famous' guests, but endeavour not to ask them all the usual questions. Or be sensational. Or deep dive into a single issue, or try to be prescriptively instructional. Instead, I would create a format that everyone would have to follow. Namely that they would nominate a favourite film, book, song, place and possession for us to discuss. And there would be no exceptions. No matter how famous you are, the format would be king and couldn't be changed. If you wanted to choose a TV series not a film, you couldn't. If you couldn't decide on one film . . . Tough, you had to.

So, in 2019, I recorded the first episode of The Five of My Life, with Todd Sampson. The premise of the show was – and, four years later, still is – for the guest not to talk too much about the choices themselves (interesting though that can be). It is instead to use the choices as a device to talk about an area of the guest's life. Hopefully, a different area for each choice.

When I ask them why they chose their film, if they say, 'Because I like it,' they are a moron. Oops, there I go again – temporarily slipped into default critical mode. What I mean to say is that what I'm after is something more like 'Because it reminds me of my violent father' or 'I watched it when backpacking around Russia with my secret gay lover' or whatever. Then, with a quick hop, skip and an interviewing jump, we can hear about and examine their unconventional childhood or complex sexual awakening.

I don't want the conversation to be chronological or comprehensive. It's not supposed to be a rehashing of their CV. If we don't talk about what the guest is known for – great. It's an excellent opportunity for them to reveal a hitherto unknown side, or indeed to correct a misunderstanding about themselves.

Most importantly of all I don't want to just interview people I admire, like or agree with. I want to interview all sorts from every walk of life. People I have never heard of. People I suspect I wouldn't want round for dinner. People I vehemently disagree with. And treat them all with respect, kindness and generous curiosity. Whether you feel there is a little bit of Good in everyone or not, I choose to believe everyone is at least 'half an hour interesting'. And if they don't come across as such, it's my fault as an interviewer – not theirs as a person.

Attempting to park my old default setting, I try to empathise with all my guests, look for the good in them and their choices, and bring the best out of them. And rather wonderfully, I've found it works for me. I have ended up genuinely liking almost every single guest. Including a whole host of names my previous judgemental self would have written off with a censorious eye roll.

It's been remarkably useful in giving me a kinder, gentler view of my fellow humans. And one I can adopt in my real life, not just when I'm in the studio with headphones on. Now when I see someone pushing themselves forward with potentially dubious credentials, I try to look for the positives in their message and remember that they, like everyone else on this planet, is merely doing the best they can with what they've got. And on those occasions when I interview someone who has unarguable talent and hard-earned success, I make the conscious decision to choose admiration, not jealousy or resentment, as my response.

Thankfully, apart from my own selfish personal development, it appears to be working on the 'enjoyable thought-provoking' front as well – and it turns out that everyone *is* 'half an hour interesting'. Guests on the show have included prime ministers, Olympic gold medallists, CEOs, religious leaders, comedians, celebrity cooks, film stars, newspaper editors, world champions in various fields. And to a man and woman, their choices – and the stories they lead to – have been fascinating.

At my age my interests would typically be narrowing, but fabulously the process of researching my guests and their choices has exploded the variety, and quantity, of my cultural consumption. I often find myself about to listen to a rap song, or watch a film I've never heard of, with a sense of dread. And end up loving it. And then disappearing down a rabbit hole of further related research.

One guest chose a film about Zen Buddhist monk Thich Nhat Hanh, and my interest was so engaged and sustained that Kate started to worry that I was off to a monastery.

Another – Deborah Frances-White, host of The Guilty Feminist podcast and live show – inspiringly explained her belief that you can't learn anything without failing, and that you don't have to be perfect to be a force for meaningful change.

Hugh Mackay, Australia's most experienced social researcher, argued that active listening is an act not just of love but also of courage. Every person has taught me (and hopefully some of our audience) something useful. Or, at the very least, pointed out a book, song or film worth checking out.

To my delight, a growing audience appeared to share my enjoyment of accessing the guests 'sideways' through their choices. I started to receive lovely emails every week, the most satisfying being those in which people told me they'd thought they knew everything about a particular guest only to be surprised by a '5ML' story.

One local woman wrote in saying she'd been a member of Rabbi Kamin's Emanuel Synagogue congregation in Sydney for over twenty years and learnt more about him in the half hour he was on the show than in the two decades in his synagogue. Others told us they ended up liking people they previously despised. Or that they had been moved to spend a couple of hours researching more about one of a guest's particular choices.

All music to my ears. And I suppose it was the reason why, rather presumptuously, we entered 5ML in the annual Australian Podcast Awards in our first year. Being so new and in the fiercely contested 'interview' category, we thought we didn't stand a chance.

Well, stone me if we weren't shortlisted. It felt like such a validation of what I was trying to achieve. We were up against some very successful and well-established media brands, such as The Betoota Advocate and Mamamia, so we realised we weren't seriously in the running for the big prize, but were genuinely delighted to have made it to the final six. It solidified my secret, ludicrously lofty founding vision of releasing an episode every three weeks until I die. And then handing the show over – hopefully to one or other of my kids – to keep the 5ML brand alive for future generations.

The long odds on us winning sugared the pill when I realised my visit to Mum in Queen Camel meant I couldn't actually attend the awards night itself. I sent my younger son, Harry, in my place, assuring him all he had to do was be polite and grateful to any judge he might meet who had shortlisted us, and kick back and generally have a nice evening drinking as much free booze as he and his girlfriend could lay their hands on.

I was therefore totally blindsided when on the night itself I answered my mobile in my Mum's house, only to have to hold it far away from my ear as an ecstatically drunk Harry screamed down the phone, 'Fuck me, Dad, we won! *We won!*'

'No way!'

'Way!'

'Really?'

'Hundred per cent. I had to go on stage and make a speech!'

He wasn't joking, and it wasn't the drink talking – we had actually won. The judges rather nicely wrote in their award presentation that '5ML lifts the interview to another level and gives the listener a unique perspective'.

To top it all off, as podcasts are purely an audio medium and therefore no-one has a clue what I look like, I'm informed that when Harry took the stage and gave his speech it started a minor ripple of 'Hasn't he aged well?' Thanks, Harry.

I *love* doing them.

Learning a new skill at my age is such a privilege. I'm constantly trying to improve as an interviewer. And it isn't just the talking with fascinating people and the research that goes into it – the whole process is wonderful. Heading in to the middle of Sydney to the media company who do them for me, Southern Cross Austereo, is a joy.

Given my life and career choices it's been years since I've had a daily routine of going into a large office block in the CBD full of intelligent, friendly, enthusiastic, creative people like I used to when I was working in advertising. I find it such an energising environment. Everyone is so young. I'm comfortably twice the age of my producer and I love it. And him.

We record the episodes on the fifteenth floor of a large tower block, which means more often than not I share the lift with a gaggle of vibrant, chatty, fashionable types on my journey skyward. I secretly enjoy these elevator rides, vicariously enjoying their youthful banter. It's not always smooth sailing, though.

On one occasion, I picked up a coffee for both myself and my producer on my way to the lift. When the lift doors opened, a tall smiley hipster got in and said, 'Fifteen, please.'

'Sure,' I replied, pressing the button with an elbow as both my hands were holding the steaming coffee cups.

She then looked me straight in the eye and with an engaging angelic smile said, 'You're double fisting today?'

I stared at her like a stunned mullet. *Double fisting? Bloody hell, this is next level inappropriate and overfamiliar,* I thought.

But then again was I being too old fashioned? 'Err . . . can we say that even in these liberated times?' I replied in my best friendly nonjudgemental Bill Nighy 'I'm with you but a bit uncomfortable talking extreme sex to a stranger forty years my junior' tone.

She pointedly looked down at the cups in both of my hands, then back up at me. 'Double fisting – *two* coffees,' she replied with a look of utter disgust.

However much I protest otherwise, Kate maintains that this story says something deeply disturbing about my perverted state of mind. Irrespective of the rights or wrongs of my initial reaction, though, a fifteen-floor lift journey has never before or since taken so buttock-clenchingly long.

Clearly my personal growth has a way to go yet, but leaving my coffee faux-pas aside I feel blessed to have fallen into this opportunity. One of my guests – Remo Giuffre of TED Talks fame – memorably told me on the show that his core life philosophy is simply: 'I choose to live a life of passion.' After my long, often-joyless corporate career, four short years hosting 5ML has reaffirmed my belief in the merits of that approach.

4

Friends

I WORRY THAT I haven't got enough friends. Nor the right type of friendships. I should make it clear that I love all the ones that I have got dearly – and cherish those friendships. I don't stomp through life like an affectionless meat robot. I actually have quite a varied social life that I'm deeply grateful for – cards nights, pub trivia, book club . . . each with a different group of wonderful people. Plus a whole host of other fabulous families, couples and singles Kate and I share dinners and fun with in between.

No, what I'm talking about here is a deep nagging feeling that, for a variety of reasons (and I know many men who sacrificed personal relationships on the altar of their career and feel the same way), I've failed to develop a group of intimate male pals. A pack of mates that I hang out with on a regular basis for riotous japes and meaningful, helpful conversations.

I don't mean a small fixed set of homies like in *Sex and the City* or *Friends*. I'm not convinced that having an unchanging exclusive group of friends is the best way forward. I'd always welcome new ones. The more the merrier.

Yet, and I feel embarrassed to admit this, it somehow feels like a failure of manhood not to have this group. And not to know how to develop one. I look at examples of what it's supposed to be like to be a man, be it in beer ads or TV shows, and it just doesn't chime with my experience. Unlike Homer, I don't have a Moe's bar where I can regularly meet up with my version of Barney, Carl and Lenny.

Many of the men I know don't have my issue. I envy them their long-standing close friendships from early schooldays. They're connected to where they grew up both physically and emotionally. Yet others – including me – aren't. Being sent to boarding school at an early age meant all my school mates lived miles away from each other. And that was in England, so in my case that means another country entirely. Our family location was always changing, as Dad's job meant we moved home every few years. And giving up alcohol twenty years ago, whilst a life saver, has added to the friendship issue, given the central role it plays in so much of male socialising.

As well as my inability to create a fixed set of male friends, I've failed to develop the gift for comfortably staying in touch with people I like. I've never been sure of *how* to – again a situation made worse because, for the last twenty years, 'meeting for a drink' has no longer been an option.

I find it awkward to contact friends simply because I like them and want to spend time with them. I feel there has to be a reason to call beyond friendship – something to ask or do. This has sometimes led to me inventing reasons that make the situation awkward, or alternatively meant that I never call and therefore haven't nurtured the friendship.

Kate, on the other hand, is a natural at it. I sometimes feel I wouldn't have any friends at all if it wasn't for her. It's something I'm delighted my own kids don't suffer from either. As far as schooling was concerned, I was determined they would have a completely different experience to mine. Having them in the local government school round the corner from where we live is one of my happiest memories. Seeing some of the friendships they developed there surviving different high schools, unis and early jobs is a source of deep satisfaction. I truly believe a number of them will be friends for life.

With my insecurities about my friendship situation long being a chip on my shoulder, I was ecstatic when, at the start of my advertising career in the mid-1980s, I bumped into one of my best friends from junior school as I was walking down Charlotte Street in London.

'Nigel!' someone yelled from across the busy road.

I looked up to see a man running towards me through the traffic, dodging the cars.

'Fuck me. Tim!' I replied when I saw his face.

I hadn't seen Tim for ages. Despite having been in the same class and rugby team for years at prep school, we'd gone to different high schools and then universities and – for the reasons explained above – just gradually fell out of touch.

'What are you doing here?' he asked.

'I work around the corner at the Health Education Authority.'

'Doing what?'

'Oh, just advertising.'

'Me too – I work for Saatchi and Saatchi,' he said, pointing at their office building behind us.

'No way!'

He hugged me. It felt good. Like we had never lost touch. Tim couldn't stop, though, because he was late for a presentation. We arranged to meet after work at the Fitzroy Tavern.

It was one of the most magical nights of my life. The Fitzroy Tavern came to prominence in the 1950s and '60s as a meeting place for artists, intellectuals and bohemians. Now it was a favourite watering hole for ad industry workers. Packed to the rafters every night with young people with too much money, freedom and energy – all looking for a good time after a hard day hustling.

And here I was in the thick of it with my old mate Tim. Not just my old mate, but now my new mate all over again after so many years. Since moving to London in 1986 to start my career, I'd worried about being lonely. However, maybe being here wouldn't isolate me from old friends, but reconnect me with them instead.

That night we sat in a booth amongst the noisy backdrop of that pub and laughed and laughed. And laughed. Hours spent reminiscing and catching up. We were the last to leave and parted with another heartfelt hug and an agreement to meet again at the weekend. As I travelled home on the Underground, I couldn't help smiling at my good fortune of reconnecting with my old friend. I resolved to never lose touch with him again. Having done so once – given the circumstances – was maybe understandable. Twice would be careless.

I still had a bounce in my step when I got to work the next morning. It even affected my telephone manner.

'*Yello,*' I chirpily remarked as I took the first call of the day.

'Can I speak to Nigel Marsh, please?'

'Sure can – speaking.'

'Nigel, it's Tim's boss calling from Saatchi and Saatchi.'

'Hey! I gather he told you what happened yesterday?! Amazing coincidence, it had been so long, we literally . . .'

'Nigel, I have to interrupt you. I'm calling with bad news.'

'Oh.'

'Tim is dead.'

'What?'

'I'm sorry – there's no easy way to say it. Tim died in a road accident on his way home last night . . .'

Thirty-five years later I still find it hard to think about, let alone write or talk about. It was so unspeakably hideous. My shock, distress and guilt obviously pales into insignificance when compared to the effect on his poor parents and family. A cruel, cruel waste of a wonderful young man who had so much to offer.

It was also such a brutal reminder of how lucky we are to have our friendships. And how it is a massive error, unwittingly or otherwise, for men in particular to neglect the friendship side of the ledger as they build careers and families.

For those who don't find it natural, we should make a point of proactively putting in the effort to cherish and nurture our friends, for as long as we are blessed to have them – however awkward some of us might find the process. With apologies to the people in Sydney I've invited to play chess . . .

5

The third trimester

MAYBE I'M WRONG in wanting people to view the term 'old' as something positive. Perhaps it is simply too much of an ask – the word is now irretrievably negative when applied to people and we need a new one instead. Or, to put it another way, we need to rebrand 'old age'. The best alternative I can think of is 'third trimester'.

The term has considerable merits. In pregnancy the third trimester is something to value, enjoy and prepare for, despite the inevitable tiredness, emotional intensity and physical discomfort. Why not have a third trimester in life generally?

In many cases, life can actually be split into three parts. The first, when we're children, dependent and being educated in the broadest sense. The second, when we're doing all the heavy mid-life lifting, building a career, forming partnerships, raising children, striving for some sort of financial security. And the third . . .? What about the third? Why can't it be a good thing?

I passionately believe that it's possible. But I think you have to redefine what 'happiness' looks like and means to you in this last life stage. And what worked in your second trimester (maybe ambition, relentless hard work, competitiveness, overwhelming focus on career, etc) might not be fit for purpose in your third.

Indeed, your circumstances judged by the criteria of the previous trimester might appear tangibly worse – failing health, lower income, less status, etc – yet with the right attitude it's possible to be more joyful and grateful than ever before.

I feel that for many of us this doesn't come naturally and it's necessary to proactively and mindfully develop and nurture a third trimester attitude. In fact, it's a tragic waste not to, because one of those inevitable and sad aspects of getting to this age is the premature passing of friends.

As a young adult, if you're lucky, you tend not to know many friends who have passed away: incidents like Tim's being thankfully rare. But as a sixty-year-old, even if you're lucky, it's inevitable you'll know several. Be it through road accidents, disease, suicide or otherwise, there will be a number of people who you used to eat and laugh with and cherish who are no longer with us. Who won't get to experience their children growing up, sit their grandkids on their laps, travel to places they had dreamed of visiting, make the difference and contribution to the world they craved to, or simply lie in bed on a Sunday morning with their partner of many decades counting their blessings.

Those of us alive are the lucky ones – we have options. It's not a disappointment or disaster to get old. It's a privilege. And a privilege not granted to everyone. Many far more deserving than me – and you – aren't granted a third trimester. With this perspective I feel a personal responsibility to make the most of my old age. Not whinge about it. We are *fortunate* if we get to experience the challenges the third trimester brings. Because, let's face it, unless you believe in a heavenly afterlife or reincarnation, however bad we may feel those challenges are, they are a damn sight better than the permanent dirt-nap alternative.

6

480 hours

ONE OF THE parental responsibilities that evolves in the most dramatic of ways is your role when it comes to driving. For decades I was basically an overworked, unpaid, part-time taxi driver, constantly ferrying four young kids to all points of the city. And don't get me started on weekends, when they all had away matches for their various sporting teams.

Then suddenly in your third trimester, bang – you aren't driving them. They are driving *you*. There is this terrifying transition stage between you driving them and them driving themselves alone in which you have to sit powerless in the passenger seat whilst they learn to drive. In Australia you have to do this for *120 hours*. For each child. And keep a detailed log of every trip: where you went, how far, and how long it took you. I know many people who, because they couldn't face the huge time commitment involved, filled the logbook with invented trips to avoid the entire scary process.

And that's their business. No judgement here, but I'm not one of them. I stuck to the process rigorously. Much to the hilarity of their friends, I made my long-suffering children do every single one of the 120 hours and log it all in their respective logbooks. I didn't do this with a sense of moral superiority. It simply stemmed from an unshakeable belief that putting a sixteen-year-old behind the wheel of a motor car – no matter how well behaved and mature they might be – is like handing a drunk chimpanzee a loaded machine-gun with the safety catch off and releasing it into a crowded shopping centre.

Tragically, I know too many people who have been killed or maimed on the roads, and anything that can lessen the risk of my children killing themselves – or other people – gets my support. If you have four children like I do, that means signing up for 480 hours of white-knuckled, hands-on-ceiling, foot-on-the-phantom-brake, 'Lady-with-pram!' screaming terror, combined with 'Not-this-fucking-street-again' mind-rotting boredom.

As the first cab off the rank ten years ago, Alex had it worst. My friends call me Grandad for the way I drive, and it would be fair to say I am slightly cautious. In over twenty years in Australia I have never got even one penalty point on my licence – and I always drive five k's below the speed limit. It sends Kate up the wall. But hey, 'As the only non-drinker, if you want a lift back from this party we're going at my pace' is my appallingly self-satisfied attitude.

So, Alex got the full Grandad treatment. I used to take him to a local carpark and spend hours yelling, 'Feed the rope when steering,' and 'Check the mirrors' every ten seconds.

It's a wonder he can drive, poor bastard. I remember my dad teaching me and I was completely incapable of not stalling or crashing while he was my teacher – yet when anyone else was, I could manage completely fine. I cringe when I look back at how awful and inept a teacher I must have been and marvel at Alex's patience and resilience.

Which makes his younger brother's experience all the more exceptional. When Harry turned sixteen, he was yet to start the 'Grandad feed the rope' torture as he was doing work experience on a friend's farm six hours west of Sydney. Driving lessons with his father were planned to commence on his return home.

I intended his first time behind the wheel to be the same as his brother's – in a carpark going at five miles an hour, whilst I lectured him confusingly about how you feed the steering wheel through your hands like a rope and never cross your arms.

An excited phone call from the farm at the end of his first week shattered that aspiration.

'Dad, it's brilliant here!'

'Excellent. What've you been doing, mate?'

'I've been in the sheep sheds for the first two days – you wouldn't believe the swearing! Dad, do you know what they call –'

'No need to tell me, mate. What about the other days?'

'Well, on day three Howard got me to help him do some maintenance at the back of the farm.'

'How was that?'

'It was good. Made a change. Howard is so nice. And I drove!'

'You what?!'

'I drove.'

'But you can't drive.'

'Can now.'

'Err . . . what do you mean?'

'Well, Howard drove me and him three k or so across the fields to the back of his property to do some work on this water hole, but when he got there he realised he'd forgotten the pump he needed. So he asked *me* to drive the ute to the farm to pick it up and bring it back!'

'Didn't you tell him you hadn't driven before?'

'Yeah, of course. He just said there was nothing to it. Then he moved the seat forward so I could reach the pedals, showed me where the key went, told me to watch out for holes in the track, and then said he'd get the site prepared while I was gone. It felt rude not to do as he asked.'

'That's ridiculous! How did you go?'

'Bit nervous at first, but I soon got the hang of it.'

'What did Howard say when you returned?!'

'"Thanks for getting the pump."'

'He didn't mention the driving?'

'Nope.'

'At all?'

'Well, not then. But the next day it was raining, so he asked if I'd drive the kids to school for him.'

'You're making it up! I don't believe you. Off the property into town?!'

'Yeah. Promise. It was great. I picked them up as well.'

I have never felt more of a city ponce. To date, neither Alex nor Harry has had an accident, so it shows you what I know. And maybe, just maybe, I could do with taking the stick out of my arse and adopting a little bit of the rural 'no fuss, don't overthink it' attitude if I ever have to teach anyone to drive again. Not, of course, that they will be able to avoid the 'feed the rope' lectures entirely. After all, someone has to maintain standards.

7

From little things, big things grow

RELENTLESSLY CHIPPING AWAY at completing the kids' driving logbooks reminds me of another daily project that has become a major part of my third trimester. One that similarly irritates the kids, but has a wider benefit than getting them their driving licences.

Since 2011, I've picked up at least three pieces of other people's rubbish whenever I have walked the dog. This change of behaviour was the result of a meeting I had with a bloke named Tim Silverwood, to discuss the environmental initiative I was part of called Earth Hour. Tim had recently launched his own project, 'Take 3 for the Sea', and it seemed sensible to compare notes and share learnings.

As he explained 'Take 3 for the Sea' to me, I was struck

by its simplicity and remember jealously thinking how much more actionable and potentially helpful it was than Earth Hour. Whilst Earth Hour was successful in terms of raising awareness globally, 'Take 3 for the Sea' is something you could do every day. Something that – like all those small trips in the car eventually leading to 480 hours – might just eventually make a meaningful dent in the seemingly irreversible damage we are doing to the oceans.

I'm a passionate believer that small actions can have enormous impact – especially if done repeatedly for a sustained period of time. So for the last decade or so, much to my kids' embarrassment, I have always picked up at least three pieces of litter every day.

I've slightly adapted Tim's original idea in that I do it from places other than just the beach. Let's face it, not many are lucky enough to live near a beach and the concept shouldn't be limited to those who are.

Actually, I usually pick up more than three pieces. Hell, if you've bent down to pick something up and another three pieces are within reach, why not pick them up as well? Truth be told, and much to Kate's – not just the kids' – concern, I've started *looking* for litter. I pick it up in parks, shopping malls and at the bus stop. Anywhere, in fact, where I can see both a bin and rubbish. It just seems like the community-minded thing to do.

When you read about those huge islands of plastic rubbish floating in the Pacific or see chilling film clips of soupy ocean water created by microplastic beads that will never fully decompose, it's natural to feel overwhelmed. It's easy to believe there's nothing you personally can do that would help address such an enormous issue.

Looked at in this light, picking up someone else's bottle top, plastic fork and cigarette butt from the park can appear utterly pointless. But I actively choose another perspective. One of my favourite quotes is: 'The biggest mistake humans make is thinking because they can't do everything, they should do nothing.' *Of course*, the three pieces of rubbish I picked up this morning was, so to speak, a mere drop in the ocean. Or more accurately, merely another three things not dropped in the ocean. But if you factor in yesterday's three pieces and the three from the day before – and so on – a different picture begins to emerge.

Based on a conservative estimate of me picking up five pieces of rubbish every other day, the numbers are quite surprising and encouraging. Over the years, there are 10,000 fewer pieces of rubbish clogging up the environment than if I hadn't bothered.

'Take 3 for the Sea' is a mass participation movement, though, so imagine that twenty other people have been doing it with me in my suburb (again an extremely conservative estimate, given that it represents less than 0.2 per cent of the local population) and that twenty others have also done it in their suburbs. Say at Mirnubia. And Blacktown. And Marrickville. And Penrith. Those 100 people in those five locations alone would have stopped one *million* pieces of rubbish from polluting our planet.

Call me naïve but, while trying to stay realistic, that makes me proud and hopeful at what a little bit of collaborative community action can achieve. Because, of course, it shouldn't be limited to 100 people in five areas – it could easily be millions of people and hundreds of thousands of locations around the world. I find the possibilities truly inspiring.

When I pick up my three or five or whatever pieces of rubbish, I don't think of the next 10,000 I'm going to pick up – I think of the direct connection to the millions of pieces that others will prevent from spoiling the environment. As someone far wiser than me once said, we're all part of an inescapable blanket of mutuality.

Of course, 'Taking 3' shouldn't be used as a justification for complacency – it should be viewed as a floor, not a ceiling, to one's contribution to society. But millions of pieces of rubbish cleared up is, as my dear granny used to say, 'Better than a slap in the face with a wet fish.' And, irrespective of any help it might give in preventing the globe's destruction, life is simply nicer for everyone when neighbourhoods are not covered with detritus.

This goes to the heart of a change that occurs in many people's third trimester. Looking back to my first trimester, I realise my motivation was heavily weighted towards proving myself. In my second trimester, as I matured, the focus moved more towards *improving* myself. In my third trimester I find I'm focusing more on how I can best make a contribution to society – both now and for future generations.

But we needn't be martyrs or puritanical about that contribution. In fact, over the years I've found there is a powerful personal benefit from my seemingly altruistic 'Take 3' behaviour. One of the more popular TED Talks of recent times is 'If You Want To Change The World, Start Off By Making Your Bed Every Morning' by US Navy Admiral William McRaven.

It's a great speech, which compellingly explains how this simple daily action helps set you up right to attack the day, secure in the knowledge that you've at least achieved *something* – however small. At the risk of one-upping the admiral, to my mind 'Take 3' has all the same benefits, plus the added satisfaction that the daily action benefits people other than yourself. It can give you an added feeling of connection, to go along with the sense of being in control of your day.

US President George W. Bush once said that the only thing he knew every morning when he woke up was that he wasn't going to have an alcoholic drink that day. Leaving aside the fact that this might go some way to explaining his questionable political legacy, I feel it is actually relevant here in the same way. Similarly, if I'm ever asked back to do another TED Talk, I think I'll do one entitled 'If You Want To Change The World And Feel Good About Yourself, Start Off Every Morning By Knowing That Whatever Else You Might Or Might Not Do, You Are Going To Pick Up At Least Three Pieces Of Rubbish That Day'.

Kate says I might need to work on shortening that title, but hey, it's only a rough draft, a starting point – much like three pieces of rubbish a day . . .

8

Cancel Christmas

THE CHRISTMAS AFTER my fiftieth birthday was an especially memorable one. For all the wrong reasons.

Kate's father, John, had been increasingly poorly throughout the year. Towards the end of it, she took a call from her mother saying she really needed to come over. Upsettingly, it looked like his final days were very near.

It's the one unsolvable problem of living in this fabulous country: distance from ailing parents. Distance from non-ailing loved ones has largely been addressed by mind-bending technology like FaceTime. As a young child, when I was at boarding school in England whilst my parents were in America, I had to wait two weeks for my blue self-adhesive airmail letters to get to Mum and Dad and then another two for their reply, telling me their thoughts on my latest sporting or academic underachievement. In more recent years, I could FaceTime my parents in their small rural village in England from the side of a swimming pool in Sydney, turning the camera around to show them the twins playing a water-polo match. As I said, mind-bending.

So, staying in touch with parents back home wasn't the issue. However, being physically present during their dying days very much was. It's such a long and expensive trip that the realities of the family budget and looking after the kids and holding down paying work prohibit you from suddenly, or constantly, disappearing for weeks at a time. And timing it right is nigh on impossible, as these things rarely go to plan.

The benefit of still being married after all these years (yes, yes, amongst all the other wonderful benefits) is that one partner (me in this case) can at least keep the wheels turning at home whilst the other one jumps on the first available flight.

Which is what Kate did. So far so good. Until I took a call from my brother – telling me that our dad had passed away.

Kate was still in the air, so it made for the strangest of conversations when she called upon landing at Heathrow.

She'd left a message: 'Hey, sweetheart, I've just arrived. I'm waiting for my bags, not a bad flight, we were actually half an hour early. Call me if you're still up.'

I called her back immediately.

'Darling, there's been bad news.'

'Oh, sweet Jesus, is it the kids?'

'No, no, the kids are fine.'

'Oh, thank God – what's up?'

'Dad died.'

'Dad's died?! Oh, that's too awful. If only I'd come earlier. I've got to go, must call Mum – she'll be distraught. I should have been by his side, not sitting on a stupid plane. I can't believe –'

'No, sweetheart, *my* dad's died.'

'Your dad?'

'Yes, my dad.'

'What do you mean?'

'Well, he died.'

'But it's my dad that's supposed to be dying.'

'I know, but still my dad *is* dead.'

'Oh, Nigel, I'm so sorry. What are you going to do?'

'Get on a plane.'

'What the hell are you going to do with the kids? And the house? Who's going to feed the dog? Haven't you got two speeches booked for next week . . .?'

It was all a bit surreal, but after twenty-four hours of frantic domestic and business emergency admin, get on a plane I did. And barely two days after I arrived, Kate's father passed away as well.

Both our fathers dead in the same week, and buried in the next – the last week before Christmas. Mine on the Tuesday, Kate's on the Friday. Oh look, quick, it's time to put the sodding turkey in the oven.

Definitely more *woe, woe, woe* than *ho, ho, ho* for us that year.

And there was plenty of reflection. Losing your dad tends to do that to you. Especially if your spouse has just lost theirs as well. And never mind us – what about our fabulous mums? A century of marriage between them and now facing the rest of their old age without their life partners. It was so hideously cruel. And what possible use was I going to be to them, living so far away on the other side of the world? It didn't seem to matter so much when our parents had each other.

Thankfully, both Kate and I have siblings who live near our mums who were able to do an amazing job, but in some ways that just added to my guilt. Me swanning around on the Sydney coast, whilst my brother uncomplainingly did all the parental heavy lifting.

The funerals themselves were moving occasions, perfectly fitting for the amazing men – gentlemen – they were honouring. I'd met Kate at Abbott Mead Vickers (an advertising agency in London), and we came from almost identical backgrounds, with each of our fathers having had long distinguished careers in the British Armed Forces. Hers was in the Airforce, mine in the Navy. The parallels were eerie, in fact – both were named John, both had served in the military, and now, after eighty-odd years of entirely separate lives, they were both being buried in small Church of England village graveyards, only miles and days apart.

The speeches were tender and reflective of the wonderful careers and lives they had led. They were dutiful men who were brought up to serve – not just in the military sense, but overall. To put themselves last, provide for their families, place their lives on the line to protect their country if asked, and with the philosophy of trying to be a living example to their kids and grandkids.

They came from an era in which you judged someone by their actions, not their words. Where one of the worst sins possible was to boast of your achievements or complain of your ailments. Attention-seeking of any kind was an anathema and wouldn't have entered either of their heads.

They were resilient and calm, the mountains around which the occasional storms created by various children and grandchildren could swirl. Never flinching, simply listening before providing calming, soothing, wise advice. Advice rooted in years of life experience and delivered with unsentimental, but deep love.

Listening to the eulogies, it was hard not to feel a surge of personal failure amongst the sadness. What the hell had I done with my life that could even remotely measure up? A career advertising cars and jeans and the like seemed pathetically trivial. And whining about finding meaning and yearning for enjoyable balance (as I have been known to) felt so self-indulgent and, well, *wet* when compared to their 'man up and just get on with it' examples.

And they weren't just wise and steadfast – they were fun. Such fun. Holy crap, I can remember weekends filled with gales of laughter with both of them. Hilarious, drink-fuelled Christmas games, country walks and sparkling dinner-table banter and micky-taking. And what great grandads. More open, available and relaxed in that role than their upbring-ing and generation allowed them to be as fathers, they were adored and admired as Ganfie and Grandpa.

Although their lives had many similarities, their final years couldn't have been more different. Kate's dad displayed an almost-superhuman refusal to amend his lifestyle in the face of the advancing years. Taking great delight his whole life in smoking (much to Kate's mum's annoyance) and hot-air ballooning into his eighties. When he was 'retired' from piloting hot-air balloons after a particularly startling landing (for him and his passengers), undeterred he simply went out and got a sail boat instead. Brilliant.

In contrast, my dad's equally joyful lust for life was tragi-cally cut short by the scourge of Parkinson's and dementia. An appalling fate for both him and Mum to endure.

Irrespective of any similarities or differences, now they were both gone. Joined in death like we will all be one day. And the day wasn't too far away if, like me, you were rapidly approaching sixty. As I said – made you think.

It was in this reflective mood that I set about dealing with an administrative matter on my return to Sydney. It was utterly trivial in the grand scheme of things, but important to attend to nevertheless, as a considerable amount of money was at stake. Our original plan for Christmas had been a holiday overseas, not two funerals in the UK. As a family of six, it was no small financial commitment, but one we were prepared to make as Kate and I sensed it might be the very last holiday away we'd have all together as a tight discrete family unit, before kids started to leave home or wanted to bring partners etc.

Now we were back in Australia, the only thing left to do was to claim on the insurance for the cancelled holiday. It was Kate who had taken out the policy, as I have to admit I've always thought of insurance companies as Satan's Agents on Earth and every policy they sell as merely a con to trick honest working people out of their hard-earned cash under false pretences. But I was very happy to be proven wrong in this case. Just maybe I had been unfair and insurance companies came into their own in precisely such extreme circumstances as this?

'Hi, I'd like to claim on my policy for our cancelled holiday,' I said to the friendly woman once I'd told my story to a number of people and eventually got put through to the right department.

'We just need to establish where he passed away, sir. When you say the West Country, are you referring to Western Australia?'

'Ah, sorry no, I mean the West Country in England. Somerset, to be precise.'

'Thank you. I'm afraid the policy doesn't cover your holiday if the death occurred overseas.'

'I'm not sure I understand. What exactly are you saying?'

'The policy provides cover if the holiday is cancelled due to a close family member's death, if that death happens *within Australia.*'

'But that doesn't make sense. Why would it make any difference where he died?'

'It's quite clear in the policy, sir.'

'So if Dad had died in Wagga Wagga, Wollongong or Wyalong, you'd pay out, but because he died in Sherborne, you won't?'

'Yes.'

'Seriously? But why on earth would it make any difference where he passed away?'

'It's just the policy terms, sir.'

'But they seem a little random, unfair and cold. Not very human, really. It feels like we spent hundreds of dollars on insurance precisely in case of an unlikely and unforeseeable scenario like this, yet you're getting out of paying up on a technicality. Your website says, "We're all about meeting our customer's needs," but this feels slightly contrary to the spirit of that statement.'

'We have to stick to the rules.'

'I'm not sure you do, actually. I think you're free to do exactly what you wish. After all, you set the rules in the first place. Surely, given our immigrant population, it's obvious millions of Australians will have elderly parents overseas. It's as if you've deliberately designed the rules to avoid helping them. Is there any way you can look at this case on its merits? It couldn't be clearer, if you look at the spirit of the policy and our claim.'

'I'm afraid not. Your father died in the wrong place.'

'So am I right in saying that if I'd known my dad was going to die and had flown him to Sydney purely so he'd pass away in Australia, you would have refunded our holiday in full?'

'Yes.'

Madness.

To be clear, this wasn't some little-known company – this was the second-largest insurer in Australia and the official partner of one of the Big Four banks. Our bank who had recommended them. And financial institutions wonder why they are hated.

9

Self-Help

IT'S ONE THING deciding to write a book. And choosing a theme and a title. It's quite another to control how it is received and perceived when you've finished. The harsh reality is once you've sent off the final edit to the publisher, it's no longer yours. The end product is out of your control. It, and therefore you, are at the mercy of the vagaries of the market. The publisher, critics, bookshops, Amazon and readers will decide its fate.

Apart from inducing a slightly shameful desire in this author to therefore *never* finish – and just enjoy the part of the process I can control; the writing – there is nothing wrong with that. But I do have one post-publication issue that I am uneasy with.

I'm conflicted about ending up in the self-help section. Which is where my books so often seem to be categorised in store or online. I've long had a love-hate relationship with self-help. The industry seems too often to be all tip and no iceberg, crowded with people of dubious credibility, self-appointed experts who, on closer examination, often have zero compelling experience or training to speak of. And in many cases, they exhibit behaviour that provides a convincing rationale for them to be ignored entirely.

So it's fair to say I have a pretty negative view of the whole self-help genre. And yet . . . and yet I *love* it.

I've read hundreds of self-help books. And benefited greatly from many of them. How can this be possible given what I've written in the last few paragraphs? My friend Mike maintains that it's possible for something to be rubbish and great at the same time – that indeed many things are.

I found this out when I confessed, to his horror, that I adore the film *Love Actually*. I suppose he has a point – it is pretty shite. Arguably quite appalling gender politics, definitely cliched and shudderingly heavy handed. But I *still* love it. So that's my rather flimsy defence for my galloping hypocrisy in slagging self help off, yet loving it at the same time.

I'm painfully aware of all the charlatans, bad advice and unrealistic promises of magical results, but I still come back to the essential power of the genre. I'm told a number of Catholics feel similar emotions about their institution. The truth is that the core advice constantly retreaded in most self-help books *is* useful. And properly implemented can be transformational. Taking small steps, changing your mindset, not letting fear hold you back, raising your expectations, etc, etc, might not be new suggestions, but that in no way invalidates their power.

As Somerset Maugham said, all the core truths are too important to be new. It's to be expected that these truths are constantly repackaged and represented in a fresh manner, and by a relevant source, that makes them accessible and appealing for a new era and new audience.

I'm a firm believer that you can learn from other people's stories and thoughts. Indeed, I feel it's essential that we do. But I'm an equally firm believer that you've got to be very careful who you listen to.

A journalist challenged me on this point a few years ago when she asked me to name four of my favourite self-help titles for an article she was doing on the genre. Looking at the press cutting now, I see I chose:

Viktor Frankl – *Man's Search for Meaning*
Gordon Livingston – *Too Soon Old, Too Late Smart*
Ellen Langer – *Mindfulness*
Marcus Aurelius – *Meditations*

It's a list I'm still comfortable with today. But leaving aside the titles themselves (wonderful as I think they are), it is the authors themselves who point to an interesting lesson. The first is a Holocaust survivor and founder of logotherapy. The second, a decorated Vietnam veteran *and* protestor, twice-bereaved parent and psychiatrist with over forty years' clinical experience. The third, a professor at Harvard and the first woman ever to be tenured in Psychology at that university. And the fourth – well, the fourth was Roman emperor for twenty years and the most significant source of our modern understanding of ancient Stoic philosophy.

The point I'm trying to make here isn't that you have to be a Roman emperor or Harvard professor to have the right to a voice. Many of the most inspirational and instructive stories down the ages are of 'ordinary' people. But maybe before you resort to taking instruction from an Instagram influencer, you'd be better off to first search for someone who has lived a life, and had a career, that makes them worth listening to more than, bless their hearts, the latest YouTuber or TED speaker. The four authors named above also, importantly, all have humility – a quality somewhat absent in the purveyors of those '10 tips to be as clever and successful as me' books you see in the airport.

So where does my loving and loathing of the self-help category leave me? I don't really know. As I said, I'm not trying to write a self-help book. I'm just looking back over my life and forward to my sixties and telling a few stories as honestly as is possible for a repressed military child in need of a ton of therapy.

But the simple fact remains that I'd like what I write to help some people in some small way. I'm certainly not doing it for the money. If you're publishing a book in this day and age to make a living, you've clearly 'missed a meeting', as they say in business. That party is over. To adapt one of my favourite quotes about poetry: publishing a book is like dropping a rose petal into the Grand Canyon and waiting for the echo. Especially if you only do it once a decade.

My writing might not feed the family, but I have had enough emails over the past twenty years to show me that a few people have found some of my thoughts comforting and useful. I've replied to every single one of those emails – and, it's slightly embarrassing to admit, have printed them all off and filed them away in my study. Who knows, one day I might even re-read them. Whether I do or I don't, the point is I *love* it when someone says I've helped them.

So, with no little apprehension and a lot of humility, however much I might protest otherwise, what follows *could* be described as self-helpy. And therefore, to my horror, will probably end up in a few self-help sections.

A lot has changed since I last put finger to keyboard for my book about turning fifty. Not 'a lot' in an *Angela's Ashes* 'Here comes my misery memoir' sense, or 'a lot' in terms of the heroic *127 Hours* tale (the story of a guy who cut his own arm off with a pocketknife so he could crawl to safety), which might provide the content for an inspirational against-all-the-odds story.

Just 'a lot' in terms of normal life as you progress through your fifties: both parents passing away, children leaving school, children leaving home, seemingly everyone divorcing, children coming back, career heights receding into the distant past, new friendships formed, jobs come and gone, even more Australian prime ministers come and gone, family finances depleted, travel undertaken, Ash Barty winning the nation's hearts, herb garden planted. Just stuff. But it hasn't all been change. I am still married, writing, and living in the same house in Sydney.

And I haven't touched an alcoholic drink since 5 April 2003. Well, not deliberately, anyway.

10

Queen Camel 1

IN EARLY 2019 I received a call from my brother saying our mother was extremely unwell and had been taken to hospital in an ambulance. To my eyes, there aren't many bad things about living in Australia, but, as I've explained, this is the worst. Thankfully, my brother lived with his family barely 15 kilometres away from Mum. Whilst this was wonderful for her, it did mean that Jonathon shouldered an uneven portion of the load in an unavoidably unfair division of labour.

Many of our friends in Australia have elderly parents in the 'home country', be it the UK, Greece, South Africa or Canada, and face the exact same issue. Increasingly so at our age, as our respective parents start to nudge ninety. A conversation with one of them – Alan – was incredibly instructive.

'Nigel,' he said, 'don't fall into the trap of attempting to plan it so you're there, holding your Mum's hand, when she takes her last breath.'

'Blimey, mate, that's exactly what I'm planning,' I replied.

'And that's normal and understandable. It's a mistake many people in our situation make.'

'Why's it a mistake?'

'Because you should plan instead to spend time with her *before* her last moments. Meaningful time. Now. When you have the chance. Important and lovely though it is to be there at the very end, you can't guarantee you'll be able to arrange it so that you are. And even if you can, she might not even be conscious or aware of your presence at that stage. Think of how you can have the maximum positive impact for her. It might just be that a week when she's well – if she gets better – is far more appreciated than the day when she's dying.'

I thought about what I would want when, and if, I get to Mum's situation and concluded that having my kids visit and spend time with me – proper time – would be my deepest desire. I booked flights later that evening.

Never one to knowingly do things by halves, I booked for a whole month, not a week. I embraced the uncertainty of the timing, fully aware that she might be dead by the time I arrived. Or out of hospital and in robust health. Or relapse the very day I took off at Heathrow so I'd have to jump back on a plane the moment I landed in Sydney. But if I left it until I was certain of the right timing, I would never go. So rather than dither, I committed.

A friend of mine recounts a story of when he was going through the same dilemma. He's a religious chap and was discussing it with his priest.

'She's very ill, Father. The trouble is, I'm enormously busy at the moment. I have so much on – at work and at home. To go away this month would be terribly difficult. So I'm thinking of planning a trip later. In the summer.'

'Tell me, son,' the priest replied. 'Exactly how many mothers do you have?'

Ouch.

11

Wellness porn

WELLNESS PORN. WHAT is it? I use it to describe the peculiar habit, and industry, that has sprung up of people selling their fabulous lives. Or the illusion of their fabulous lives. The unrealistic depiction of your aspirational lifestyle for other people's entertainment and motivation – or often a desperate search for personal validation.

Truth be told, enough is currently right about my life (for which I'm extremely and everlastingly grateful) that, if I so wished, I could paint a misleading picture of sun-kissed, beachside, wedded bliss. I might use the type of photos you see on the cover of those diet books – slim woman in ripped, stone-washed jeans holding the handlebars of a bicycle with a wicker basket full of organic veg, hair blowing artfully back in the wind as she grins manically to camera.

But it's just so forced and inauthentic. Those books aren't selling the recipes, they're selling the lifestyle. Buy this book and you too might be able to have the wonderful life that the author looks like he/she enjoys. But the trouble is, I know a number of those people. Whilst I like them, none of them actually have that lifestyle – it's all an illusion. And that's not to mention the endless tragic stories of celebrities who suicide at the height of their 'happiness' and fame.

Leaving aside the cancer fakers like Belle Gibson, I don't blame them for how they market themselves or their product. It's not their fault – or even in some cases their idea – that they feel the need to join in, as so many others are doing it.

It's like those annual family update cards which arrive at Christmas and fool no-one as it's obvious to all – including the sender – that they're simply a poorly disguised humble-brag narrative of the good things to have happened over the past year. ('Big discussions ahead for us this Christmas as Francesca can't decide between Oxford or Cambridge'.) Or my all-time favourite, complete with buttock-clenchingly embarrassing exclamation mark, 'Charles is going to use the Upper East Side apartment next year whilst doing his internship at The Met So convenient!'

They remind me of the Charles Dickens line where Scrooge says, 'If there's one thing more nauseating than Christmas, it's a happy marriage,' these annual updates combining both topics in the same card. But to be fair to the people in the latter case, I'm told by a friend in New York it's actually a cultural thing in America. While in the UK and Australia it would be seen as unacceptable big-noting, in the US it's just what you do and apparently not bragging at all.

I'm prepared to give them the benefit of the doubt. And let's face it, it would be a bit weird to have a picture of yourself on the cover of your Christmas card or diet book having just got out of bed, and not combed your hair or wiped the sleep from your eyes. Or writing a Christmas update saying your career has flatlined, you find your partner Olympically irritating, and you're really worried about your kids, one of whom has dropped out of uni and the other who has a drug habit. 'Francesca can't decide between smack and coke' might be nearer the truth, but lacks a certain something, whatever the cultural nuances of the country where you live.

It does make me think, however, about a wider issue than Christmas card etiquette. I have long believed that an essential component of happiness is to seek contentment in the average, rather than constantly expecting the exceptional. But more recently, I've come to believe that there are actually more rich, valuable, genuinely useful and lasting lessons to be gained from so-called mediocre people with average lives than from the 'exceptional' ones the media so often laud.

Study the sporting hero and billionaire entrepreneur if you like, but you might actually learn more from your work colleague who has never won as much as an Olympic bronze or sold a corporation for squillions. She has 'just' brought up a contented, functioning family, maintained a rewarding, long-term, intimate relationship and always got on with her neighbours. Pathetic? Heroic and inspirational, more like.

It's not just 'mediocrity' that's got a bad, unhelpful press – it's melancholy. And in some ways, this is more damaging. Wellness porn gives the impression that life is all about – or should be all about – joy and happiness. Which is obviously bollocks.

Inevitably, life is full of grief and loss. All the people we love will eventually disappear, if we ourselves don't disappear first. We'll spend years striving for things that we likely won't get or achieve, and if we do we'll soon be disappointed, as we decide to strive for something else instead. Most, if not all, of our relationships will be with people who never truly understand us. Everything we enjoy and crave is bad for us. And nothing we're ever likely to achieve ultimately matters in the grand scheme of things. How much do you know about your great-grandparents' lives?

All of the above is fine. Welcome to Planet Earth. But wellness porn gives us the wrong expectations and, in my humble opinion, contributes to the mental-health crisis. Because to be occasionally sad or melancholic in the face of all the above should be viewed as *healthy and normal*, not a condition that needs to be cured. Or something to be ashamed of or worried about. In many cases, sadness is the right, healthy and helpful emotional state in the face of life's difficulties and disappointments.

Call me a bluff old traditionalist but, for example, I'd suggest that buoyantly fist-pumping at your parents' grave side, whilst parroting inspirational Nelson Mandela or Dalai Lama quotes, is not the best method of coping with grief. Sombre isn't always bad. It is often entirely an appropriate response to life's events and a damn sight more healthy than constantly striving for some permanent state of cheerfulness, based on never-ending 'Christmas card success'.

I'm not arguing in favour of walking around under a permanent cloud. On the contrary, I'm a huge fan of positive thinking. As long as it's reality based and appropriately timed. Nor am I in any way wanting to make light of genuine

clinical depression – which obviously needs qualified professional attention. I'm simply suggesting that by the time we
reach sixty, most of us realise that suffering and sadness are
an essential part of what it means to be human and we have a
better chance of making the most of our third trimester if we
embrace, not deny, that fact.

But some people *like* the unrealistic fantasy. So the media
give it to them. And there is hell to pay when they don't.

12

The Sydney Skinny

I REMEMBER WHEN the talented actress Jamie Lee Curtis posed for the front cover of a woman's magazine, *More*. It was 2002 and she was at the height of her fame – based in large part on her appearance. And, more specifically, how she looked in a skin-tight leotard – which in case you don't remember was stunning. Like how a teenage boy would draw a cartoon fantasy woman. In fact, one of her more famous films was called *Perfect* and required her to basically wear nothing else but a leotard the whole movie.

In this case, however, she decided to 'keep it real'. In a laudable attempt to help other women feel better about themselves, she wanted the shot to show everyone how she really looked. So she posed in her granny pants displaying her tummy rolls, leaning over to one side, which accentuated her back fat and side muffin.

And was she praised to the skies for such an honest and well-intentioned front cover? Was she fuck. She was lambasted and swamped by hate mail. People writing in to express their outrage that she had 'betrayed' the illusion that they'd willingly bought into – and desired. They didn't want her to look real. They wanted their aspirational heroes to stay aspirational – as a form of escape and entertainment.

This is fine to a point. As long as people know it's a fantasy and that really all the photos are retouched and that she was in hair and make-up for hours before the shoot. And that if they saw how she really looked in the morning (which they don't want to), she obviously wouldn't be 'front-cover worthy'.

The trouble starts when people forget it and become deluded about the reality of human existence. Which is why I founded a thing called the Sydney Skinny – an annual nude ocean-swimming event held at Cobblers Beach.

In my last book, *Fit, Fifty and Fired Up*, I explained my motivation:

> Wouldn't it be the most uplifting, hilarious, cleansing, pure, grounding event ever? Every year we could do some good by raising money ... while having a boatload of fun. It would be a way to throw off the straitjacket of modern over-commercialised life, remind people of the simple things and what's really important in life. A chance to be utterly authentic and stick two fingers up at all those ludicrous, airbrushed images of bodily perfection in the magazines. A safe opportunity to rebel and be ever-so-slightly naughty ... just imagine how joyous an

experience a 1K bare-butt communal swim in the world's most beautiful harbour would be.

But whatever benefits people might get from doing the event, for me and Kate, there are the added benefits of running it. One of those is the gorgeous people we've met. The event tends to self-select and attract people with fabulous values and a certain something about them. Many have become close friends.

In the early days back in 2012, when I was looking for a corporate sponsor for the first event, I had countless rejections from big companies. It was hardly surprising really, given I was selling a public nude swim that was entirely unproven and yet to take place. There was just so much that could go wrong.

Would anyone turn up? Would it be sleazy? Would there be a scandal? What about safety as, let's face it, isn't Middle Harbour basically an underwater shark highway? And as for the press: how on earth would we be able to control them, so I could keep my promise that no-one would have their tufty bits on the nation's front pages or TV screens?

Company after company would listen politely to my passionate pitch that we were on a mission to make the world a slightly nicer place. That the event had nothing to do with promoting nudity – it was, in fact, all about courage, acceptance, joy and charity. A supportive celebration of all that's good in this life. That it was globally unique and perfect high-profile proof for any brand that they actually stood for something, beyond the 'increasing shareholder value' pronouncements. That it would be ideal, for instance, for Nike to show 'Just Do It' hadn't become an empty slogan, or for Dove to show that their 'Campaign for Real Beauty' wasn't simply another cynical attempt to cash in on women's insecurities.

I had high hopes for Dove. They'd recently spent millions on a campaign urging women to focus on the important things ('Real Beauty'), rather than the superficial. To resist the false images and fear that advertisers use to manipulate women into buying expensive products in a futile attempt to reach some unattainable version of youth and beauty. To be self-confident and healthy, not an insecure wannabe stick insect riddled with botox and plastic surgery.

So you can imagine my surprise when their response to my pitch was, 'Oh no, Nigel, here at Dove we are not about the beauty of women as they are – we're about what they can become.' Rightio, my mistake then.

Time and time again I would visit companies whose advertising or mission statement would proclaim values and objectives almost identical to the Sydney Skinny's, and time and time again I'd get polite nods and then what my friend Lisa calls the 'slow no'.

It wasn't so much the lack of sponsorship support, it was the shocking lack of authenticity. Forget my swim, it was just so depressing that none of these companies seemed to mean what they said. Or even mind in the slightest when that was pointed out. It was as if they expected no-one to believe their expressed values and mission statements were anything other than advertising bollocks, and I was the stupid one for believing for a second that Nike might actually be an adventurous company or Dove genuinely cared for boosting women's self-esteem. It was a pretty brutal insight into the real values of corporate Australia. Until, that is, I met James Ajaka.

When I announced in *Fit, Fifty and Fired Up* that I intended to set up the Sydney Skinny, I included a line about my hope that a company such as Nike or Nudie would come on board to sponsor the event, as in both cases the fit seemed so perfect. But while Nike, like Dove, told me where to get off, the Nudie experience was altogether more pleasant.

I set up a meeting with the company's then-CEO James Ajaka. When I finished my passionate pitch, he said, 'I love it!'

'Really?' I replied, hardly daring to believe my ears.

'Yep, it's sensational. Perfect, in fact. Next year is our tenth anniversary and we've been looking for ways to mark it. We've had a succession of agencies pitch ideas to us, and all of them have been lame or off the mark. Concentrating on our name, rather than our mission. But how you describe your hopes for your event is precisely aligned to our "Creators of Good" company purpose.'

And he was right. 'Creators of Good' was so in keeping with what I wanted to achieve for the Sydney Skinny, it could even have been the slogan. It looked like I'd found my perfect partner. But I didn't want to let him down.

'I have to be honest with you about the value you'll get from the sponsorship,' I told him. 'I haven't a clue. No-one might turn up. Or hundreds might turn up, but we might get no coverage. Alternatively, we might get millions of dollars of coverage, but no mention of Nudie. It's just a huge leap into the unknown.'

But James didn't seem too concerned. 'Your job is to create something wonderful,' he said. 'My job is to leverage it.'

Perfect partner indeed.

It was such a relief when hundreds of people turned up for the inaugural swim in 2013. And because everyone seemed to really enjoy it and told their friends and family about it, the next year even more people came. Every year the pattern was repeated until we had thousands of people doing it and a hardcore community of Sydney Skinny loyalists spreading the word.

It's difficult to do justice to the joy of the event on paper. You simply have to be there to understand it. Reading emails, social media posts and press articles of people describing the positive, supportive experience they've had on the day, and the lasting beneficial effects it has had on their lives overall, is truly heartwarming.

Nudie went on to be our presenting partner for the first three years of the event. Over this time, they never put a foot wrong or tried to meddle with or change the event in any way. I've worked in marketing and branding for over thirty years and I've never been part of a better partnership.

Our experience with the corporate world was replicated in other areas. It was as if the Sydney Skinny was a bullshit meter that exposed inauthenticity. This was never more apparent than in the 'industry' of body image.

Even more shocking than my corporate meetings were my conversations with a number of self-proclaimed spokespeople for better body image for women. These people talked a good game. But when push came to shove – when I suggested they should take part in the swim – they ran a mile. 'Oh, I couldn't possibly – no-one wants to see *my* flabby belly.' Kind of missing the point, methinks.

I wouldn't mind if these were ordinary people quietly going about their business, but these people had set themselves up as high-profile advocates advising other women to ignore the idiotic societal pressure and to love their bodies as they really are. Yet all too often, the pitch was merely a shallow 'Do what I say, not what I do.' (One exception to this depressing hypocrisy was Taryn Brumfitt – founder of the wonderful Body Image Movement.)

Kate and I have been humbled, touched and inspired by the wonderful people who have become part of the Sydney Skinny community – like Layne Beachley, the seven-times world surfing champion; Charlie Teo, the brain-cancer surgeon; or my friend Max, who is wheelchair-bound, yet has done every single Sydney Skinny.

But that's not to say it's been easy. There have been a number of less than helpful surprises – ranging from the merely humorous to the downright depressing.

After the first event I was contacted by the police, who wanted to know if I wished to press charges against a woman they'd arrested earlier in the day.

'A streaker?' I enquired, perplexed.

'Yes sir, at 9.23 am a Mrs Thompson landed her water-craft at Cobblers Beach, having motored over from Clontarf, stripped off all her clothes and ran up and down the beach completely naked whilst waving her hands in the air.'

'But it's a nudist beach.'

'Well, yes.'

'And a nude event.'

'True as well. But the fact is we have procedures to follow, so I have to establish if you'd like to press charges.'

'Of course I don't want to press charges,' I explained. 'It sounds like she should be given a medal not a penalty, but I wouldn't mind if you could give me her contact details. She seems to have misunderstood the nature of the event somewhat . . .'

Another more delicate surprise in the second year (when we moved to having twelve – not one – waves of swimmers to cope with the increase in numbers) was the difference in how various people behaved once they came out of the water at the end of their one-kilometre swim.

As they arrived on the beach, each competitor was handed a sarong to protect their modesty and keep as a memento. Most people immediately wrapped it around themselves and wandered off to find their clothes to get changed. This was important as although it's obviously a nude event it is absolutely not about being *seen* naked or *seeing* other people naked (there's nothing wrong with that, but it isn't what the event is about).

Some people, however – usually men – took their sarong, said thank you, stood at the finish line, turned to the ocean to review with satisfaction the course they'd just completed, and proceeded to dry their hair with the garment. It wasn't a crime but it might have been mildly confronting to some of the more timid participants coming out of the water from later waves. It was nothing we couldn't resolve the next year with a gentle 'Please move away from the finish line to avoid crowding', but an unforeseen issue nevertheless.

More surprising, and depressing, though, was the email we received during preparations for our seventh year. It was entitled 'Confused and Disappointed' and read:

> I was shocked to notice on your website that at this year's Sydney Skinny there will be a fundraising BBQ. The World Health Organization declared in 2015 that 'sausages are carcinogenic to humans' and I therefore can neither attend nor support your event.

There were two possible responses to such an email. One was to politely point the sender to the more recent survey conducted in 2019 by Dalhousie University and McMaster University in Canada, which, after reviewing twelve trials involving 54,000 people, concluded that 'we did not find any statistically significant, or even an important, association between meat consumption and the risk of heart disease, diabetes or cancer'. And then to mention that there would also be a variety of organic vegan and vegetarian options available on the day and that we hoped she would consider attending, or donating, despite the BBQ.

The other way to respond was to say, 'What the actual fuck? Really? *That's* your take-out from reading about the swim? Not that we are all about joy and courage and acceptance. Not that we'll raise tens of thousands of dollars for cancer research. Not that hundreds of people will have one of the best days of their year in a communal celebration of all that is good in this world. But that we have a BBQ? *A fundraising BBQ that will be staffed all day by a cancer surgeon and his team.*

'Meanwhile, all you can do is send a snippy, virtue-signalling, scientifically incorrect email. You need to seriously think about the lens through which you see life and your impact on the world, else you may just be heading for a bitter resentful old age shouting at pigeons in the park, full of regret that you've achieved nothing of positive value with your years on this earth.'

I still wonder if I was right to send the first one.

13

Fifty shades of grey

BBQ WOMAN, AS we'll call her, got me to thinking about a trend that has become increasingly noticeable recently – the seeming inability of people to have a calm nuanced debate with people they disagree with. And to stay friends with them if agreement isn't reached.

I don't know whether this is the effect of social media, falling educational standards or simply a growing sensitivity to it as I enter my third trimester. People seem not just comfortable but *keen* to rush to extreme and oversimplified pronouncements and sweepingly vicious personal judgements. Pompously certain of the rightness of their view, without the slightest amount of proper research or debate, and happy to dish out the most mean-spirited malice to anyone who might disagree with them.

Why bother getting properly informed when you can enjoy the bliss of sloganeering on social media. And without ever being challenged either, as you refuse to be friends with anyone who holds even a slightly diverging view. These people don't indulge in thoughtful debate and respectful listening.

They are impervious to rational argument and hostile to any dissent. I try not to let it bother me – I just bite my tongue and let the latest over-claim or oversimplification wash over me and not spoil whatever social occasion I happen to be at.

I've lost count of the times I've heard someone from one 'side' dismiss *everyone* from the other. Sweeping generalisations like 'I can't understand how anyone with a heart could ever vote conservative'; or 'The trouble with socialists is they're economically illiterate and anti-business'. Really? All of them?

Both views are just so lazy and unimaginative. I know a number of smart and successful business people who are socialists. And, quite frankly, after fifty-eight years on this planet if you believe the left has a monopoly on compassion, you simply haven't been paying attention.

But it's not just an issue when discussing politics. It seems to be an issue when discussing *anything*. The climate, Covid, animal welfare, Ukraine, the republic, the rights of oppressed minorities – even trivial matters like entertainment. It doesn't matter what the topic is: the problem is the overall mental approach.

There seems to be a growing inability to countenance anything but the most basic generalisations. And then with a quick hop, skip and jump, eagerly get into personal insults based on identity politics. I was once accused of having a problem with Indigenous artists because, when asked, I was honest and admitted I hadn't particularly enjoyed a recent book by an Indigenous writer.

I usually try to just let it go. But every now and then when someone says something particularly irritating, or if I'm in a mischievous mood, I can't resist.

'God, the patriarchy shits me,' a delegate remarked to me at a recent conference. 'I can't believe the state of the world. If only we could get a few women into power.'

'I'm not sure it's that simple,' I replied, 'or that having more women in power is going to sort *everything*.'

'Of course it would – if only a woman could ever *get* into power, that is.'

'Oh, come on. There have been loads of women in power.'

'Rubbish! Name one.'

'The Queen.'

'The Royal Family doesn't count.'

'Fair enough. Margaret Thatcher.'

'Not a woman.'

'What?'

'She's not a woman. Doesn't speak for her gender.'

'Err . . . okay – Theresa May.'

'You're only using UK examples.'

'Julia Gillard.'

'Proves my point. Done in by the patriarchy.'

I went on to mention Gladys Berejiklian, Jacinda Ardern, Angela Merkel, and Sanna Marin and her all-female cabinet in Finland, but she wasn't having a bar of it.

'I was thinking about a broader canvas than just politics, Nigel. Big businesses are all run by men.'

'Granted, many are,' I replied, 'but the last multinational

agency network I worked for had a female CEO – both globally and locally.'

I added that the highest-paid CEO of any industry in the whole of Australia is also female, as is the head of my bank, my agent, my publisher, the head of the ABC and the presenter of the radio programme I wake up to every day.

In short, despite the ever-present risk of being accused of being a mansplaining misogynist, I argued that her analysis of the current gender balance amongst Australia's most powerful was maybe a little simplistic.

To be fair, what she probably meant was: 'I reckon the world would be better off if more women were in power.' Well, I *hope* that's what she really meant – a reasonable, defendable statement and one that I happen to agree with. The trouble is that we might need to be more measured in our language and careful with our logic if we want to be taken seriously – or have a positive impact.

I'm not trying to make a point about politics or any specific topic here. I'm talking about how we debate and relate to each other generally. Surely we can all be a bit better? And by all, I include myself, as I'm not immune to the siren call of tribal belonging achieved by oversimplifying and virtue signalling.

But surely it should be possible to raise our game enough not to write off a charity swim because it has a BBQ, or claim that everyone who disagrees with us politically is either stupid or hard hearted? I'm not sure there are literally fifty shades of grey, but I do think with most issues it's worth at least making the effort to try to find some middle ground before retreating into a black or white position.

Also, what is it with all the 'unfriend me if you disagree with this' posts on social media. Really? I like my friends because I like them. They are kind. And interesting. Some are funny. I couldn't care less if they have a different position on fiscal policy or forestry management or whatever.

Who knows, maybe I could learn from listening to their position. Maybe, God forbid, I'm wrong and *they* are right. Or, perish the thought, perhaps we could respectfully agree to disagree, secure in our broader friendship and the knowledge that no-one has a monopoly of wisdom on anything. The belief that you can be friends with people who have differing views and interests seems to me to be one of the cornerstones of a civilised society.

As I say every year at the starting line of the Sydney Skinny, what unites us is more important and powerful than what divides us. And Australia forgets that at its peril. As I enter my third trimester, I resolve to be aware of the insidious evils of recreational outrage, tribal cliches, comforting victimhood and lazy, cruel, blanket condemnation, and will attempt to hold myself to a higher standard of empathy, kindness, intellectual curiosity and humility.

Even when I next meet a swimmer mortally offended by sausages.

14

Memory Lane

As I GET older I increasingly have moments when something triggers a wave of emotionally reflective nostalgia. It could be a song on the car radio, a smell in the kitchen, a picture on Facebook. The smallest and most unexpected stimulus can send me off into the most intense, and extended, reverie.

A couple of years ago we stayed in a friend's holiday house over the Australia Day weekend. They're a family we've known since we migrated here over twenty years ago. They had always been welcoming and kind — Sally inviting us for numerous dinners when we'd just arrived and knew no-one, and David patiently helping me train to do the Bondi to Bronte swim all those years ago before *Fat, Forty and Fired*.

As they weren't going to be using their holiday place that year, they'd generously offered it to us. It's a modest residence on the mouth of the Shoalhaven River at Greenwell Point. Unusually, since they had long since left school, we had all of our children with us and I was looking forward to it enormously.

On the drive down I had soppy visions of a lazy schedule full of beach cricket with the kids, romantic walks with Kate and evening BBQs with the whole family together. However, the moment I walked into the house, I wasn't looking forward I was looking *back*.

In the sitting-room was a battered chaise longue. Fuck me – *our* chaise longue. The one Kate used when she was feeding the twins. The one we had given David and Sally two decades ago. When the shipping container with all our belongings had finally arrived from England, we couldn't fit the chaise longue into the house we were living in, so we'd offered it to them.

I put my suitcase and rucksack down and sat on it, running my hands over the worn material, memories and emotions flooding through me. So much had happened in the time since. Crystal-clear images of the twenty years of our adventure building a family life in Australia started scrolling through my mind: until, that is, Kate came in, jokingly yelling, 'Bloody hell, what's taking you so long?! Come help finish unpacking the car, Shirker Tenzing.' (The name my family gave me after years of my perceived dodging of domestic chores.)

'Recognise this?' I replied, pointing to the chair.

'Oh wow – I remember us buying that back in London.'

I took a picture of Kate sitting on the chair and texted it to David, with a surprised emoji, saying, 'I remember this!'

Moments later, he texted back: 'That's nothing – take a look in the bedroom.'

I showed Kate his reply and we walked into what would be our bedroom for the weekend to investigate. Nothing stood out. Until Kate lifted the edge of the doona off the floor to reveal the basic wooden slatted bed underneath.

'No way!' I gasped.

Sure enough, though, it was – the bed we'd bought in Camden market in North London way back before we were even married. However, we'd got fed up sleeping on a mattress on the floor, waiting for our shipping to arrive in Australia, and had bought another one. We'd given this bed to David and Sally at the same time as the chair.

The memory movie in my head went into overload. Never mind the last twenty years in Australia, it was now playing images from thirty-five years ago.

'I can't believe we're going to sleep in our old bed again,' I mused.

'*I* can't believe you're ever going to finish unpacking the car, Nigel,' Kate replied.

'There are more than a few good memories – not to mention children – made on this thing,' I said with a smile.

'Eww, Dad!' Grace exclaimed in horror, as unbeknownst to me she'd just walked in behind us.

'Ah, sorry sweetheart, your father can be so inappropriately revolting,' Kate said to Grace, before turning to me and tenderly saying, 'Stop being such an old softy. Finish the unpacking.' She paused and added with promising ambiguity, 'We can reminisce later.'

The weekend was everything I had dreamed of – relaxed family time. A framed picture of us there two decades ago with David and Sally was hanging in the house, adding to the nostalgic theme of the weekend. We kayaked as an entire family around Goodnight Island – not being bothered by the fact that we had to share paddles, as there were six of us and only five of them. We even took the dog – much to Mattie's initial distress and then delight. We played cards, watched the Australian Open, ate more barbecued sausages than the Sydney Skinny BBQ woman would consider medically advisable, went for lazy walks and played beach cricket in the evenings.

The whole experience reminded me of Gandhi's sentiment that if you live your life right, you can enjoy it twice. Once in real time and then again as a memory. It's something I believe and am constantly mindful of. Just as our old chair and bed were powerfully evocative of our life before Australia, I felt in Greenwell Point I was not only having the time of my life but at the same time laying down powerful memories that hopefully I'll get to enjoy again with Kate twenty or thirty-five years from now, when something (maybe even this book) triggers recollections of that wonderful weekend.

However, an incident with my daughter Eve reminded me that this attitude is best kept as a personal pleasure. After I'd finished the unpacking, and still buzzing from the emotions of seeing our old chair and bed, I walked to the local butcher with her to buy supplies for the weekend. As we walked along the banks of the Shoalhaven River, I peppered her with memories and questions about our previous visits.

'Do you remember coming here with Grandpa and Omi?' 'How about that time we played Pooh sticks at the bridge?' 'Wasn't it hideous when both you and your sister were sick in the car after we'd given you too much chocolate on the way back from Honeymoon Bay?'

On and on, I wittered. As we approached the butcher I pointed to the river winding past the oyster beds and asked, 'Do you remember what that river is called?'

'Nope,' she replied.

'Surely you do. You've swum in it a thousand times.'

'Nope.'

'Go on, have a think.'

'Daaad.'

'Come on, you banana, you must remember. At least have a guess.'

She turned to me and, with a 'butter wouldn't melt' expression, said, 'Err, okay . . . is it the River I Don't Give A Shit?'

Harsh, but fair.

15

J is for Jemima

As WELL AS being sensitive to memory triggers, I'm also a sucker for coincidences. In fact, I point them out so often that Kate long ago remarked that maybe they aren't actually coincidences, but instead are just *life*.

'Nigel, I agree it's a lovely song and I know we used to listen to it in Crouch End, but it simply isn't a remarkable coincidence that they are playing it in both London and Sydney. It was a top ten hit and it is a music radio station after all.'

However, there is one incident that I refuse to believe is not a noteworthy coincidence. I'll let you decide.

I'm fortunate to receive a regular trickle of reader emails. They started on the publication of *Fat, Forty and Fired* and have never stopped since. I get them from all over the world. Wonderfully, often from countries I've never even visited. It was no surprise therefore when a couple of years ago I received an email from a reader in Texas. Jerry generously told me that he had enjoyed *Fit, Fifty and Fired Up*, explaining that as a father of six he related to a number of my experiences and observations regarding parenthood. He ended his message with the offer that if I ever found myself in Austin, Texas, he and his wife would very much like to invite me to their home for dinner.

So far so lovely, but not so remarkable. Until I point out that I'd never been to Austin in my life, but barely a month prior had been booked to do a speaking gig there. And that, in four days, I was flying to the city for the very first time.

It felt slightly surreal to reply saying, 'Delighted to hear you enjoyed the book, Jerry. Thank you for the offer of dinner – how about this Saturday?'

It blew my mind. I mean, I lived in Sydney for Christ's sake. What were the chances? Whether that meets your criteria for a notable coincidence or not, the trip itself proved to be one of my more memorable.

Saturday dinner at his house was agreed, and as a bonus Jerry sent me a long list of his recommendations for what an out-of-towner should best do when visiting for the first time. I'm eternally grateful to him as on the list was a suggestion to visit Barton Pools.

My favourite place on earth is Bronte Beach Pool but Barton Pools runs it a close second. It is difficult to adequately express its beauty, serenity and sheer unusualness. It's a thousand-foot-long natural pool, filled entirely from a local spring. Over three acres in size, it is set in beautiful parkland and has a natural river bottom varying in depth from one to eighteen metres. It's slap-bang on the Colorado River and when swimming you see Austin's city centre skyline just a kilometre away.

To top it off, it just so happens to be where Robert Redford learnt to swim. For me, in terms of the awe it inspires, it is nature's equivalent of the Sagradia Familia in Barcelona. But unlike the church, you can swim in it. All year round. In temperatures that rarely fall beneath 20 degrees. Heaven.

My speech on the Friday was one of those big corporate ones, to the folks at American Express. It went well, and I was relaxed and centred. How could I not be? I had swum in the world's second most beautiful outdoor pool right before it. Feeling quietly pleased with myself, I hired a car on the Saturday and drove to the address in the suburbs where Jerry and his family lived.

The house was large and new looking, in one of those nicely tended, well-off urban developments. As I rang the doorbell, I realised I knew absolutely nothing about Jerry, beyond the fact that he had six kids, lived in Austin and had read one of my books. It also crossed my mind that no-one in the world, apart from him, knew I was here. He'd only texted me his address that morning. If he turned out to be a serial killer – as opposed to the successful professional his house suggested – my body would never be found.

Fortunately, neither Jerry nor his wife, Judy, were serial killers. But their circumstances were, shall we say, slightly off the beaten track. Both were delightful and friendly. The house, however, was not quite what you'd expect, judging from the pristine outside. It was ramshackle and, frankly, a little messy. Nothing wrong with that – our house was usually a tip as well, I reminded myself.

Whilst Jerry and Judy were attentive and engaged, the kids didn't initially acknowledge my existence and seemed just a little wild. After the three of us had chatted for half an hour, they were all summoned and introduced to me.

'Nigel, this is Joseph.'

'Hi Joseph, nice to meet you.'

'And this is Jessica.'

'Hi Jessica, nice to meet you too.'

'And Joshua.'

'Hi Joshua, nice to meet you.'

Hold on, is it just me or do all their names start with J?

'And Judith.'

'And Jacob.'

'And what's your sister called – Joanna?' I jokingly blurted out to Jacob, looking at the last of the tribe.

He looked at me strangely. 'No. What makes you say that? She's Jemima.'

'Hi Jemima. Nice to meet you.'

Yep, all Js, and maybe just a bit of a biblical theme as well?

'Gosh, Judy,' I turned to their mum. 'They all have names that start with a J.'

'Yes and all unschooled,' she replied.

'Homeschooled. Wow, good on you, Judy, but how on earth do you find the time?'

'Not homeschooled. Unschooled.'

'Sorry?'

'Unschooled. They are all unschooled.'

I'd never heard of it but it turns out that unschooling is *not* homeschooling. And it's a bit of an insult to suggest to an unschooler that it is.

Unschooling, I was informed, involves an education that is not directed by a teacher or a curriculum. It's guided by the desire to let kids learn naturally by what they're interested in. Not only do they not go to school or have any formal lessons, you don't force them to learn about *anything*. Instead, you follow them. If they express an interest in planes, you leap on it and encourage and facilitate that. If it's plants or maths, same applies. If nothing quite grabs them, you don't stress, but wait until something does. If it's daytime TV, drugs and porn . . . I'm not so sure how that works.

Google it – it really is a thing, which lots of people around the world do. And I'm sure if you have naturally inquisitive children, engaged intelligent parents and a varied interesting social network it can work wonders. But I couldn't help feeling that if Kate and I had unschooled our brood, it would be no coincidence – gorgeous and much loved though they are – if they'd ended up as unsocialised, illiterate, unemployable computer-game-playing dunces.

16

The Burrow

EVERY NOW AND then Kate and I crack and admit the Sock Fairy
has defeated us. Again. As she struggles to find a half-acceptable
pair, and watches me pull on yet another outrageously ill-matched
one, she'll say, 'Sock mountain tonight. All in – no excuses.'

We then pile all the single socks into a big heap in the middle
of the carpet in our downstairs room and sit round it cross-
legged, like a family warming themselves at a campfire. The
rules are simple. No-one can leave until they have assembled at
least ten perfectly matched pairs.

On one such evening an old school friend of Alex's visited
in the middle of this process. We tend to keep an open house –
often leaving the front door hooked back on a summer's
evening. Good friends like Bucci know they're welcome to
just walk in. Which he did on this occasion, yelling hello and

walking towards where our voices were coming from. Halfway down the stairs he saw us and stopped, momentarily stunned and intrigued by the scene.

I could see him struggling for precisely the right words in response to finding his friend and his friend's brother, sisters and parents – two of them in pyjamas – all sitting cross-legged on a Sunday evening around a mountain of socks.

'Wow, err . . . gosh, fantastic – this is just like The Burrow,' he said with a smile.

I knew exactly what he meant. And it felt appropriate – a generous compliment even. Kate, on the other hand, was crushed. Still hasn't fully got over it, I suspect.

Because The Burrow that Bucci was referring to was the one the Weasleys live in in the Harry Potter books. Through my rose-tinted glasses, his remark suggested that our house, like the Weasleys', was a cosy, welcoming, relaxed, 'we're all in this together', 'all hands to the pump', lively and chaotic family home. An opinion reinforced by the fact that we made Bucci sit with us and do ten pairs of socks himself, in return for a drink.

To Kate's mind, however, his remark, though well intentioned, was a painful reminder of our home's tumbledown – or shall we say 'rustic' – appearance. Especially compared to the houses many of her friends lived in. The writer David Sedaris once described his house fitting in in his street like a rotten tooth in a mouth full of healthy white pearlers. It could equally be said about ours. Indeed, we regularly get builders' promotional 'Thinking About Renovating?' leaflets put in our mailbox.

I happen to think our home is perfect and wouldn't change a thing. But the truth is we couldn't afford to, even if we wanted to. There are, after all, real-world consequences to giving up a conventional career and 'living a life of passion'.

17

Holsten

I GAVE UP alcohol on 6 April 2003. Shampoo as well on 30 October 2006 – but that's another story. I haven't had a drink for twenty years.

I'm black and white about it. Whilst I'm happy for other people to do whatever they want, since that day I haven't let a drop of alcohol touch my lips. Not. One. Drop.

Subsequently I've become quite the connoisseur of all the non-alcoholic drinks out there. I seriously don't think there is a brand available that I haven't tasted. I constantly search for new ones online and try them all. Non-alcoholic beer, wine, spirits – the lot. It would take pages to list all the brands I've ordered from around the world and given a go. Rochester Dry Ginger, Ceder's Wild, Lyre's American Malt, O'Doul's,

Weihenstephaner, Brew Dog Nanny State, Two Valleys Syrah, Erdinger, Golden Knot Cider, Heaps Normal . . .

Kate thinks I should set myself up as an online influencer – given the decades-long, one-man testing program I have been on, believing my experience and recommendations could save a lot of people considerable time.

It's such a dynamic and ever-changing sector. The category is unrecognisably different from when I was a young man. As a twenty-year-old in London, if you ordered a non-alcoholic beer in a pub (and weren't immediately thrown out or beaten up), you'd be handed a Barbican or Kaliber. It's impossible to describe quite how revoltingly undrinkable these two brands were. Imagine if you got one of those bars of disinfectant that sit in the troughs of men's urinals. And dissolved it overnight in a warm pint of bin juice. Then carbonated it. *That* would taste nicer than a Barbican or Kaliber.

The options are now so vast – and in many cases delicious. Despite the industry's persistent failure to reliably produce genuinely enjoyable non-alcoholic wine, it's a joy that there are hundreds of brands of beer out there which actually do taste fantastic. My current favourites are UNN IPA and Heineken 0. But *all* of the major beer brands – including Kaliber – have raised their game and are light years ahead of the awful options of years gone by.

Which is why, when I saw on the Dan Murphy's website that they'd sold out of Heineken 0, I didn't think too much of it and ordered a case of Holsten 'non-alcoholic 100% taste' instead. It was a brand I hadn't yet tried, so it seemed like a good excuse to do so.

A week later, after a long hot day outside I went to the

fridge parched, pulled a cold bottle of Holsten out of the door, sat down and necked it in two gulps.

'Urgh, remind me to not buy those again,' I said to Kate as I got up to put the offending bottle in the recycling. 'They have a horrid metallic aftertaste. I'm surprised, actually. I thought Holsten would have done a better job.'

'Hold on a second,' Kate replied. 'Show me the label.'

'Sure,' I said, handing it to her.

'Nigel, this is a *full-strength* Holsten.'

Fuck me sideways if she wasn't right. It turned out that Harry – who'd recently moved back in with us – had put it in the fridge door, slap-bang next to the other Holstens I had put there. The bottles were the same size and colour and the labels the same shape. My poor eyesight, combined with the fact that there hadn't been a real beer in my fridge for years, meant I hadn't considered for a second it was anything other than non-alcoholic. And I had drunk every last drop.

So it's not actually true when I say I haven't had a drink for twenty years. I skulled a cold one on 9 January 2019.

At the time it wasn't funny. I was horrified. It seemed to me precisely the type of incident that could unravel half a lifetime of will power and recovery. The old 'Well, that shows I'm cured and can have one every now and again' delusion might enter your head and before you knew it you'd be a bottle of whisky a day fuck-up, wondering how your life went so wrong. I wasn't just horrified – I was terrified. It had been such a monumental effort to kick the booze, and I didn't want to throw away the life I'd worked so hard to create because of a stupid case of fridge-door mistaken identity.

Kate, however, didn't share my worry and was confident I'd be fine. 'Look at it this way, Nigel. I'd be far more worried if you'd said, "Chuffing hell, Holsten have nailed it. I'm going to order another crate as that was the best tasting beer I've had in years."'

I'll drink to that.

18

Coral wonderland

BECAUSE OF MY books and a TED Talk I did way back in 2010, I occasionally get asked to do interviews for overseas media outlets.

They usually reach me through my website and, if I can, I always agree. Quite frankly, I'm flattered if anyone even in my own house gives a toss what I think, so if an editor of a French TV programme or Brazilian magazine expresses an interest, I'm more than happy to give my time.

Therefore, I didn't think twice when a columnist for a newspaper in Nebraska emailed me a couple of years ago to ask if I'd do a short phone interview for his 'Five minutes with . . .' column. We emailed back and forth to work out the time difference and set a date. So far, so good. The conversation itself was short and pleasant. But a bit dull and, shall we say, *weird*.

'So, Nigel, do you still live near the sea in Sydney?'

'Sure do.'

'Swim in the ocean regularly?'

'Absolutely – as often as possible.'

'Many sharks?'

'Sorry?'

'Do you see many sharks?'

'Err . . . well, they are definitely there – it's their home after all. But no, I don't see any.'

'So you have to make a special effort to see them. What about other marine life?'

'Well, every year we see whales and dolphins. There are huge blue gropers at Clovelly and the swim from Shelley Beach to Manly is one of my absolute favourite things to do. The view is always spectacular – and different every time. The varied marine life amongst the rocks, seaweed and sand is amazing.'

'Take many photos?'

'No, not really, just enjoy the swim.'

'Save the photos for when you travel then?'

'Err . . . yeah, I take more when I'm not at home.'

The conversation went on in this vein for a few more minutes, before pleasantly wrapping up.

'How was the interview?' Kate asked, when I brought her a cup of tea that morning.

'Oh fine, but strangely he didn't ask me anything about TED, *Fat, Forty and Fired* – or even the Sydney Skinny.'

'Why was he calling then? Earth Hour or Five of My Life?'

'Nope, didn't ask about those either. He just seemed interested in how often I swim in the ocean. Wanted to know if I took lots of photos.'

'Well, Nebraska is land-locked. It makes sense, I suppose, that they're interested in the ocean.'

I didn't think about it again until a few months later. In the week after Christmas, I received a text from Beki, one of the women in my local swimming club. The text came with a photo of her young daughter standing in front of their Christmas tree, holding up a book and smiling broadly in delight. The message read: 'Look what Livvy got for Xmas! Will have to get you to sign it ☺!'

The book was blue, with a large picture of a turtle underneath the title *Close Encounters with Marine Life*. The bottom of the cover wasn't in the picture, so I couldn't see the name of the author.

Intrigued and baffled, I typed 'Close Encounters with Marine Life' into Google and up it popped: '*Close Encounters with Marine Life* details Nigel Marsh's underwater adventures with camera in hand, featuring some of his best images and many remarkable stories of his experiences with amazing marine life.'

Rightio. That explained that then. A simple case of mistaken identity. But why would both Beki and the Nebraskan editor have made the same mistake? On my website it was clear what I did and didn't do. It didn't mention marine life or photography once.

I replied to Beki's text, confessing I wasn't the author of her daughter's Christmas present. She seemed doubtful, texting back: 'But it's in your profile.'

It wasn't on my website and I didn't have a Wikipedia page, so there was only one thing for it. I typed 'Nigel Marsh' into Google. A whole bunch of stuff came up in a list on the left-hand side of the screen. Mercifully nothing too scandalous and, thankfully, it included my actual website. However, it was what came up on the right-hand side – my 'Google profile' – that was the explanation.

There, staring back at me, was a box with a large picture of me in a suit, next to five smaller pictures of me in some of my other non-corporate roles. Underneath the big picture was the byline 'Nigel Marsh – journalist'. Journalist?

At the bottom of the box were a collection of thumbnail pictures of book covers. The first three were mine, but the next five were most definitely not: *Diving with Sharks*, *Coral Wonderland*, *Exploring Shipwrecks*, *Underwater Australia*, and of course my favourite, *Close Encounters with Marine Life*.

The copy in between the photos and the books read: 'Nigel Marsh is an underwater photographer and photo-journalist whose work has been published in numerous magazines, newspapers and books around the world. Nigel has dived extensively, especially the Great Barrier Reef and Coral Sea.'

So much for Artificial Intelligence. The computer algorithms (or however they do it) that create Google profiles had somehow erroneously merged me with my diving namesake. There are far worse people to be merged with, I suppose. By all accounts subaquatic Nigel is very nice and extremely well regarded in his field.

But I do feel a little concerned that I'm forever destined to let people down when they discover I'm far less accomplished than my Google profile would have you believe. And that if any photography enthusiasts emailed me with a query about exposure, I'd only be able to direct them towards the Sydney Skinny. Not to mention feeling a little guilty for denting a reputation in Nebraska.

19

Queen Camel 2

TWENTY-ONE HOURS ON a plane gives a lot of time for reflection. Particularly if you're travelling in the cheapest economy seats next to the lavatories, and therefore have bugger all hope of getting any sleep. For many people I imagine going to spend four weeks with your mum in her house would be no big deal. For me, though, it was huge. Because the truth is, I'd never spent more than two days alone with Mum in her house. Ever.

As I've mentioned, I'd been sent to boarding school when I was five, then gone to university miles away in another city, then moved to London to start building a career, then emigrated with the family to Australia. In between, of course, I'd visited her many times – but always with family. Until recent years, Dad had been there as well. So, time alone with just me and Mum had simply never happened.

That's not to say I hadn't put serious work into our relationship – particularly since my dad had become ill, with Parkinson's and dementia. It was gradually becoming the type of relationship that I craved with Dad in his old age but was denied by his condition.

Kate was wonderfully helpful in this regard, always coming up with clever suggestions. One of her best ideas was for me to send Mum a copy of each of the books chosen by my book club the moment they'd been selected. It had become a lovely tradition. I'd tell her one was on its way, and she'd eagerly look forward to it and tell me when it arrived. Then we'd have hours of enjoyment discussing it after we'd both read it. A binding shared experience.

Another tradition was making a point of getting up in the early hours of the morning in Australia – 2 am or 3 am usually – with one or more of my kids to watch England play in the annual Six Nations rugby tournament. I would then call Mum at half-time to discuss how we were faring.

It made bugger-all difference whether England were shite, or if I was dog tired, or that Mum had no real interest in rugby. It was the tradition – and again, shared experience – that was great. And somehow genuinely meaningful.

I also began to send her random surprises – a bonsai tree for her kitchen, a head scratcher, a metal kookaburra for the garden to remind her of Australia. All provided cosy hilarity in our phone calls in the following weeks. Particularly as she managed to kill the bonsai ('The leaves have fallen off, Nidgey, is that normal?') and her cat was convinced the kookaburra was real and spent all day staring menacingly at it.

We got increasingly creative. On my most recent trip to the UK, I had organised – again on Kate's suggestion – a weekend away in a hotel for just me and Mum. Like spending a month in her house, this was something we'd never done before.

We booked a couple of rooms in a small seaside hotel in Instow, near the town where she grew up in Devon. What on earth were we going to do? What would we even talk about? At breakfast, lunch and dinner, just us two alone for three days in a row? Turns out I needn't have worried – it was hilarious and moving and, like the rugby telephone calls, somehow important.

I had high hopes that the month in Queen Camel, as well as being practically helpful, could recreate some of the same vibe and meaning. Ever since Dad had been moved to a home and been no longer of sound mind, she was lonely. His passing away had only made her more isolated and at a loss. If possible, I wanted to supply some stress-free fun companionship in the time she had left.

As the plane touched down at Heathrow, I said a silent prayer that the reality of my visit would match up to my sentimental dreams for it.

20

Mrs Singers

As MENTIONED PREVIOUSLY, I'm slightly ashamed to admit that we are one of those families that watches *Love Actually* every Christmas. At least once. It never fails to deliver. Kate *still* hasn't forgiven Alan Rickman – even though the poor bastard is now dead – for breaking Emma Thompson's heart. And she's surprised and appalled anew every year when he does. I laugh out loud at the jokes as if I haven't heard them a hundred times before. We know all the lines and spend half the film shouting them out loud before the actors on screen do: 'Err . . . would we call her chubby?', 'Eight's a lot of legs, David', 'Just in cases'. Stop me.

Not cool at all, I realise, but I don't care as it's become a fun, comfortable part of our festive family routine. Wherever we happen to be.

A few years ago, we spent Christmas with our friends who live on a farm six hours west of Sydney. Like us, they had four kids. And, like us, had a tradition of watching *Love Actually* every year. When the time came for the annual viewing, all twelve of us crowded onto their sofa and floor in front of the TV. And as usual it was great.

In this case, though, it was particularly memorable. Halfway through the film, after the famous scene where Andrew Lincoln holds up boards proclaiming his love for Keira Knightley at her front door, their ten-year-old son, who was squashed in next to me on the sofa, whispered in my ear, 'Nigel, I've seen this film hundreds of times, but I've always been too embarrassed to ask – who is Carol Singers?'

God love him. He wasn't trying to be a smart arse or make a joke. For years, he'd genuinely believed that when Andrew said to Keira, 'Tell him it's carol singers,' he was referring to a particular woman, not a generic description for a group of Yuletide crooners.

Life is full of such occasions. When you can be completely wrong, but your wrongness can work just well enough that it's not revealed to you. For years.

I'm embarrassed to admit that, throughout almost my entire adult life, I misused the word 'hiatus'. I thought it meant 'bust-up' or 'fractious argument'. And the trouble is, whenever I saw it in context – say 'The Rolling Stones are having a hiatus' – my definition worked well enough for me not to realise my mistake.

My friend Paul is driven berserk by people, including me, who constantly misuse the word 'finally' to mean the last item on a list – as opposed to its correct meaning which is 'after a long time'. But as with the above examples, the wrong definition can absolutely work in most contexts, because if it's used to refer to something at the end of a list, it's usually taken a long time to get to it anyway. So the mistake gets baked in.

In fact, in this case it's so common that, even if the style guide of *The Economist* will set you right, an internet search will quickly assure you that no-one gives a toss anymore and that 'lastly' and 'finally' can be used interchangeably. Sadly for Paul, methinks the ship has sailed on that one.

Like it seems to have with 'literally'. If that guitar solo literally blew your head off, you'd be messily dead.

I digress, but the point remains. And I think it's an important one. It's not just word definitions that, at the end of the day, don't really matter all that much. It's other weightier, more life-affecting issues as well.

We all spend our lives sincerely believing many, many things that are totally wrong – and never finding out our mistakes. 'My mother prefers my sister.' 'That bloke at work hates me.' 'My husband will love me more if I lose 3 kilos.' Whatever. For me, Carol Singers serves as a fabulous reminder that however much we feel certain about something (especially someone else), we should always bear in mind the possibility that we might actually be wrong. And not be afraid to admit it when we are, or feel shame in changing our minds.

And then we might all get on with life and each other a bit better. Finally.

21

Queen Camel 3

BY THE TIME I arrived in Somerset, Mum had been home from the hospital for three weeks and was making heroic efforts to adapt to her new routine – and reality. The terms for discharging her were that she had to have twenty-four-hour live-in care. So, it turned out I wasn't going to live alone with my mum in her house, after all. And, indeed, therefore never would. Instead, I was going to be spending a month with Mum and Dee – Dee being the wonderful, but painfully shy, nurse who had been assigned to the task by her employer, Bluebird Care.

Mum's cancer was myeloma. I'd never fully realised how many sub-brands the evil little fucker has. It turns out that you can basically get cancer of anything and everything. Breast,

lung, brain, throat, skin, bowel . . . it's a veritable smorgas-
bord. Myeloma is cancer of the bone marrow. Nice.

Mum's cancer was currently in remission but the intensive
chemo programme had knocked her for six. Myeloma is never
cured. It always comes back. And when it next did, Mum had
already decided, and unequivocally communicated, that she
wanted no more chemo. The effects of the regime had been so
uncomfortable and distressing that she knew she would literally rather die than go through it again.

As well as the cancer and the after-effects of the chemo, she
was struggling with water on the heart, a poorly functioning
kidney, limited mobility and anxiety attacks. An important
part of Dee's role was to correctly administer Mum a complex
daily regime of drugs to help manage her various symptoms.
In different doses and at varying times, Mum had to take a
cocktail of pills such as Omeprazole, Rivaroxaban, Furose-
mide, Aciclovir and Bisoprolol. (Who names these things? It's
like they were generated by a team of people at a 'who can
score the most at Scrabble' competition.)

Watching Mum swallow five pills, one after the other, at
my first breakfast with her, I suggested that if I picked her
up and shook her she'd rattle. To my delight, she smiled,
then giggled. It reminded me of the laughs we'd had over the
weekend at the hotel in Instow the year before. And gave me
hope that I could bring a bit of light relief and enjoyment to
a grim situation.

But it wasn't really a laughing matter. Mum was struggling.
Mentally as well as physically.

After that first breakfast she said to me, 'Nidgey, I'm on my
way out.'

'Good idea, Mum,' I replied. 'The rain's stopped and it looks like it's going to be a lovely day. Would you like me to drive you or shall we go with your walker?'

'No, silly. Not out – *out* out. Dying.'

She then proceeded to tell me she didn't have anything left to live for and how her carrying on felt utterly pointless. The mood wasn't helped by the stairlift breaking down so she couldn't get to her room. Stairs were beyond Mum, but on the flat she could slowly – *really* slowly – get about with her three-wheeled walker or by cruising like toddlers do – holding onto things at waist height as she shuffled along.

It brought to mind the phrase I had recently read about the 'divine circularity of life'. As a toddler, you'd be wobbly edging around the house holding onto things for balance whilst wearing nappies, and eighty-five years later you end up wobbly edging around the house holding onto things for balance whilst wearing nappies. Marvellous.

Later that morning, fighting jetlag, I made myself a coffee. I have to confess I'm a rolled-gold coffee addict. In Sydney I start every day with at least three cups. And over the years I've become a terrible coffee snob. I like my cuppa exactly to my specifications.

Visiting Mum in the past, I would drive to a local café rather than attempt to consume the unrecognisable sludge produced by the store-brand instant coffee she kept in her kitchen. Granted, it was warm and wet, but that was where the similarity with what I'd call coffee ended.

So I was pleasantly surprised to be informed by Dee that, in preparation for my stay, Mum had dug out some proper coffee. And sure enough, there in the cupboard next to an individual-size cafetière plunger thingy was a bag of high-quality ground coffee.

Surprised and impressed, I made myself a huge mug and sat down to read through the daily care notes that Dee wrote for her bosses back at Bluebird Care.

I put the lever arch file on my lap and took a sip. Yikes – I nearly spat it out across the table. Holy shit, it was revolting. It smelt like coffee, but, boy, it tasted worse than rancid arse. I went back into the kitchen to check the packet. Perhaps I'd made it wrong? Nope, there were just the usual instructions on the pack.

Hold on – what was the best-by date on the bottom? 12/02/1999. 1999?! It was almost a quarter of a century out of date.

When I asked Mum where and when she'd bought it, she said, 'Oh I didn't buy it. It was a gift Clive and Diana brought when they visited from Canada.' I resisted the temptation to point out that that had been before the turn of the last century.

When I had recovered and got myself a glass of water instead, my day didn't improve as reading the care notes reduced me to tears. Mum was clearly trying so hard but struggling to cope, God love her.

Atul Gawande, in his superb book *Being Mortal*, discusses how we as a society have to learn to better deal with the elderly in their last years. We shouldn't treat dying as an illness to be cured; instead, focusing on quality of life. Changing the goal from helping people extend their last years to helping people *enjoy* their last years.

I made a promise, there and then, that this was what I would strive to do. And made a mental note that checking the best-by dates on the food in her larder might not be a bad first step in the process.

22

The High 5 Train

ONE OF THE hard-won pieces of wisdom earned over twenty-five years of bringing up four adult children is how deluded it was of me to ever believe that, as my kids grew older, left school, went out into the world and got jobs, the worry would reduce.

Talking to friends, it seems this is a common mistake. And an understandable one. When you're in the trenches bringing up young kids, it can be so overwhelming. Poverty-stricken, anxiety-filled, domestic chaos. The list of things to worry about seems endless. It can be a useful mental device to help you get through this seemingly endless tsunami of sleepless nights, breastfeeding issues, anxious doctors' visits and teething problems to believe that it won't *be* endless. That once little Jimmy can sleep, go to the toilet, talk, feed and dress himself, walk, write and get in a car unaided, the relentless oppressive load will lessen.

And it does.

One day you'll wake up and notice that the poverty-stricken domestic chaos has somewhere along the line morphed into poverty-stricken domestic tedium. Life will get easier as they grow up and can do more and more things competently by themselves. You won't have to feed them, wipe their bottoms, rock them to sleep, get a twin pram on and off buses. But it's a mistake to equate the lessening of the domestic burden with a lessening of parental worry.

I don't want to unnecessarily upset new parents out there, but *the correlation is inverse*. The older and more competent they get, the more – not less – you worry.

And the things you worry about get bigger, not smaller. Now, rather than debate whether it's the right time to start them on solids, you agonise about whether they'll kill themselves in the car. Will they be happy? Find love? Earn a living?

But wonderfully, whilst the list grows, so do the rewards. Rather than the undeniable joy of being handed a finger painting by a toddler, you get the life-affirming, challenging bliss of spending a weekend away with an energetic, intelligent teenager bursting with potential, questions and humour. It's a deeper, more complex and enriching experience. Sharing in their hopes and fears, successes and failures as they move off into the world might cause you heart-aching levels of hidden anxiety, as you just want them to be happy and not fucked over by the world – but at the same time it's intensely moving and rewarding. And frequently hilarious.

Hearing stories about their various moves into the world of work is endlessly fascinating. Not just funny, but educational.

One of Alex's first jobs was for a sales company that would hold regular weekly JUICE meetings.

'What's a JUICE meeting?' I asked him.

'It stands for Join Us In Creating Excitement,' he replied.

'You're shitting me.'

'Seriously, it does.'

'And what the hell does one do in a JUICE meeting?' I asked.

'Well, the highlight has to be the High 5 Train,' he said, using air quotes when he said the word 'highlight'.

'I'm afraid to ask, but go on, tell me – what's a High 5 Train?'

'It's when our manager calls out a person who's done something notable – closed a big sale, created lots of leads, whatever – and asks them to "take a ride on the High 5 Train."'

'Yes, but what is it?'

'Well, everyone has to stand in a big circle and the person chosen is made to run around it twice, high-fiving us all as he or she goes.'

Lordy, lordy.

And on Grace's first day at work in a fancy restaurant in Canberra, she unwittingly laid the tables with the wrong wine glasses.

'The manager stormed up to me, Dad, and shouted in my face, and I quote, "You, and your mother, are useless fucking cunts."'

'Blimey. What's Mum got to do with anything?'

'Nothing – it just adds power to the insult. Like calling someone a skanky ho, rather than simply a ho.'

Lovely.

Then, after Harry's first week working at a pub in Wollongong, he was keen to tell me about Thursday nights.

'What's so special about Thursdays?' I asked.

'It's the $10 Chicken Schnitzel Meal Deal night,' he replied.

'Sounds good value, mate,' I interrupted, 'but, no offence, not that unusual.'

'No, it's not just the Chicken Schnitzel Meal Deal – it's also topless night.'

'Topless. You're kidding?'

'Nope. Topless.'

'You mean, the guests are topless or the staff or both?'

'Just the female staff.'

'You're telling me you work in a pub in 2020 where, on Thursday nights, the barmaids have to work topless?'

'Yep. It's quite famous locally. They advertise it as "Titty and Schnitty at the Cabbage Patch."'

Hashtag them not.

Barely a week goes by without an eye-popping story being relayed back from the frontline.

And as the stories build up, I realise a subtle shift is happening in the nature of our relationships. When they were small kids, the learning was all one way – parent imparting wisdom to child. Then, as they got older, it became more of a mutually beneficial thing. We would both learn things from each other. Now, however, I could sense we were moving back to a stage where it was more of a one-way educational flow, with the roles entirely flipped. More often than not, I was learning from them.

They were opening my eyes to how the world really was, rather than how I wanted it to be. They were exposing me to other points of view than that of my friendship group, and making me more empathic. They were intelligently debating me – and, more often than not, winning and changing my mind on a variety of issues of the day. They were challenging my jaded cynicism and inspiring me with their passion and optimism. Impressing me with their resilience. Really impressing me. In my experience, their generation being called snowflakes is far wide of the mark.

And they were always, always keeping me entertained. A recent story managed to be both funny and sad. After leaving the High 5 Train, Alex spent a number of months putting his sales skills to use raising money for charity over the phone. Despite the noble purpose of the enterprise, it was still a hard-driven sales organisation with all the behaviours that entails. Basically, you sat in a room and for eight straight hours worked your way through the telephone directory, calling every number in turn asking everyone for a donation. And I mean everyone.

I know that world from my own youth, when I also spent a few months doing tele sales. In my case it wasn't for charity, it was for exterior house wall paint. Or, more accurately – selling a consultation to have someone come round to *discuss* exterior wall paint. We were rewarded or punished solely on how many appointments we managed to book, irrespective of actually selling any paint. Or indeed if the person concerned even had an exterior wall.

When we secured an appointment, we raised our hand in a signal to the floor manager. Back in those days I didn't have to ride on the High 5 Train. Instead, the manager rang a huge brass handbell whilst shouting your name and putting a tick in your column on the whiteboard at the front of the room. Quite a bizarre feeling when you know the person who you've just arranged the appointment for lives on the eleventh floor of a government tower block that the council had recently painted, and who has no interest, money or authority to buy exterior wall paint from anyone.

But hey ho, welcome to the heady world of sales, where it's not about overthinking stuff, it's about *action*! It reminds me of one of my all-time favourite films, *Glengarry Glen Ross*, where Alec Baldwin shouts 'ABC!' – 'Always Be Closing' – at the hapless sales staff.

So Alex's job might have been for charity – RSPCA in this case – but the environment and ethos was very much 'sales'. To pay for uni, Alex was working as many hours as he could, including on this occasion Christmas Eve night.

'We were really being pushed for donations, Dad,' he explained a few days later. 'They didn't care that we were calling people and disturbing them during their festive family time. We had a target to raise a certain amount for the RSPCA by year end, and we were going to miss it if we didn't up our game.'

'And how did you go?'

'Well. Too well. I still feel guilty about it.'

'About what?'

'The last call I made that night. The phone was answered by a lovely, slightly hard-of-hearing, old lady. In a frail but pleasant voice she very politely told me she couldn't really talk, as she was about to sit down for Christmas dinner with her whole family.'

'Fair enough.'

'Yeah, but I pushed and said it wouldn't take long and that I was calling from the RSPCA with an important message. Whereupon she shrieked, "You've found my dog!"'

'Ouch.'

'It was awful. I could hear her yelling to her family, "They've found Benji! They found Benji! I knew he wasn't dead. The RSPCA have found Benji!"'

'What did you do?'

'Well, when she came back to the phone I explained to her that, no, we hadn't quite found Benji yet, but a $50 donation might just help with the search . . .'

23

Nettlebed

WHENEVER I'M IN England I try to visit Kate's mum as well as my own. Mary lives two and a half hours up the road from Queen Camel in Henley-on-Thames – a lovely part of the country. A hilariously strong character and an unfailingly wonderful host, she is a 'feeder' who insists on producing the most delicious, but ludicrously huge meals three times a day. She is great company and extremely social, and always on the go with one activity or another.

On this occasion, soon after I arrived she suggested we should visit some old almshouses in the local area. Almshouses are charitable buildings for the poor, the earliest of which were established in Britain back in the tenth century.

'Sounds good, Mary. Where are they?'

'Not far – just past Nettlebed.'

'Nettlebed? That name rings a bell – I used to have a girl-friend in Nettlebed.'

'Really? We should pop in and visit her on the way.'

'Ha ha.'

'No, seriously, we should look her up.'

'We haven't spoken in over forty years. And besides, there's no chance she'll still be in the same house she was when we were going out together in the early eighties.'

'You never know. Nothing ventured, nothing gained.'

'Mary, it's a terrible idea. And not to mention I'm not sure Kate would be all that thrilled about it either.'

'Oh, don't be silly – you said yourself it was forty years ago. What could be the harm?'

I tried to drop the topic, but Mary was full of questions about where exactly the house was and whether I'd recognise it. I told her I thought I probably wouldn't.

Eventually, the questions dried up and the car fell silent. That is, until we were driving through Nettlebed and I suddenly exclaimed, 'Blimey, there it is – May's Farm. The one on the hill over there on the left.'

Despite Mary's earlier enthusiasm, I didn't think she would do anything other than nod and say something like, 'Told you you'd remember.'

But she didn't do that. Instead, she pulled the car over sharply, did a quick U-turn, drove up the lane to the farm and parked outside the front door.

I was speechless. She wasn't. 'Go on, out you get, knock on the door. See if she is in.'

'Don't be ridiculous, Mary. I'm not knocking on that door.'

'I'm not moving the car until you do.'

'Honestly, this is embarrassing.'

'Not moving.'

'Come on.'

'No. Not moving.'

Sensing it would be quicker to acquiesce and get the whole charade over with than try to win the argument, I got out of the car. I gently knocked on the door and waited briefly.

'No-one's in, Mary,' I said, relieved. 'Happy now? Let's go.'

'Don't be silly, Nigel, you hardly touched the wood – ring the doorbell, for heaven's sake.'

I rang the bell and, to my horror, immediately heard dogs barking and someone approaching down the hallway.

A pleasant woman opened the door. Before she could say anything, I burst into a hurried apology.

'Oh hello. Listen, I'm really sorry to disturb you. I've got my mother-in-law with me,' I said, motioning over my shoulder in the direction of the car with my best 'Not my idea, I'm humouring a nutty elderly relative' expression on my face. 'You see, I used to go out with a girl called Susan who lived here forty years ago, and she thought it would be fun to visit the house, for old times' sake.'

'Hello, Nigel,' the woman replied, 'I've kept all your letters.'

Fuck me. It was Susan.

What the hell were the chances? Not just that she still lived there, but that she was at home the very moment we decided to visit? Mary was, of course, completely unsurprised.

To be fair, never has a 'Told you so' face been more deserved. Or indeed enjoyed. It turns out Susan had inherited the family farm years earlier. We had the most delightful catch-up and I've still got a picture on my phone that Mary took of us laughing our heads off together in the driveway. One of the most memorable reunions I've ever had.

And one that – after I'd got over the sheer unlikelihood of our meeting – got me thinking about my lifelong approach to 'moving on'. With my past girlfriends, it was less 'moving on' and more 'scorched earth'. Irrespective of who ended the relationship, my philosophy had always been 'over' means *over*.

Forget 'No sex with your ex'. I mean over as in 'Never talk to again'. Not in a horrid way (or that was never my intention); it's just that I was never one for the 'Let's be friends' malarkey. We needn't be enemies, but my go-to suggestion was always 'How about we never see each other ever again?' Unless, of course, my mother-in-law has a madcap idea in forty years' time.

I don't know where this approach came from – and I'm not saying it is either sensible or mentally healthy – it was just what I did. And not only with girlfriends. Looking back, I see I did it with everything: schools, jobs, industries – countries even. It was over thirty years before I went back to my old school town and that was for business reasons, not sentimental ones. I spent twenty years building a career as an advertising executive, then the next ten doing everything in my power to sever links with the industry. When we moved to Australia, it wasn't in a half-hearted way – it was with a hardcore 'Sell the house in England to eliminate any chance of going back' attitude.

A therapist would have a field day examining the root cause and motivation behind my desire to always move on, reinvent myself and totally ignore my past. I mean, what precisely am I running away from?

I've no idea, to be honest, but as I approach sixty I've come to believe it is an idiotically small-minded and limiting way to live. Why deny the past? It shouldn't be a prison that totally defines you or makes you miserable, but nor should it be something you wipe from your personal history. It should be a valuable part of who you are. It has, after all, made you who you are.

I should learn to be less extreme. It surely should be possible to move on and, at the same time, retain what's helpful from the past – lessons, memories, friendships. And a proper sense of self. I want to own all of it.

I tend to define myself by what I'm doing in the present moment – author or podcaster or whatever. But I'm also that military kid sent to boarding school at five, who worked in advertising in London and, yes, went out with Susan in Nettlebed. It's *all* part of me and I should stop blocking bits out.

My friend Rick tells me it's what the Buddhists call being a fully integrated self. That capacity to practise self-compassion, accept *all* of your life and still believe you are okay. Nearing the tender age of sixty, it sounds like an idea I should better acquaint myself with.

These are all useful learnings that I'll be taking into my third trimester. Nevertheless, they're learnings that I'll be keeping from Mary. In discussions with Kate after the meeting with Susan, it became apparent she confidently shared her mum's 'What could be the harm?' approach to past romantic partners. I trust my wife with my life but can be prone to a fragile ego. So, given her previous suitors are all dashingly handsome castle-dwelling landowners or helicopter-flying millionaire entrepreneurs, I've no desire to encourage my mother-in-law to take Kate on a similar trip down memory lane quite yet.

24

The green journal

I said I've previously written three books, but the real number is actually four. It's just that the extra one is a personal project intended for a very limited readership. So I tend not to mention it. Until recently.

Unlike my other books, which I would like tens of millions of people to read, this one has a very specific target market. Four people to be precise. I can name them all: Eve Marsh, Alex Marsh, Harry Marsh and Grace Marsh. Yep, I've written a book for my kids. And if all four of them would actually read it, it would mean more to me than any of my other ones topping the *New York Times* bestsellers list.

For the last thirty years, I've kept a journal. Still do. It's an important part of my routine, although it's not really a routine – more of an ever-present hobby in the background. It's entirely unstructured, because I might write in it five times in a day, or not pick it up for a week. Sometimes I draw in it, not write. One day I can write pages and pages of intimate thoughts, others simply jot down a funny one-liner I hear on the TV. Whether it's a speech or poem or quote that grabs me, I try to capture them all.

The actual physical journals are of all shapes and sizes. Some are bought for less than a dollar at Officeworks, others cheap giveaways from conferences I've spoken at, others gifts from the family at Christmas who are aware of my habit.

I write in them with anything I can get my hands on – pencil, biro, whatever – but my favourite is one of the two old fountain pens of Dad's that Mum gave me after he died. They're not fancy or worth anything, merely being everyday run-of-the-mill Parker pens. And they leak. But the ritual of filling them from one of the bottles of ink Kate buys me, and then blotting them with a paper towel, before sitting at my desk to write makes me intensely happy. And reminds me of my dear old dad.

To date I have eighty-seven such journals on shelves in my study. And that's where the story would end if it wasn't for the powerful and irresistible notion that struck me six years ago.

It was like a cartoon light-bulb moment. Previously I had no objective with the journals – I just got value and pleasure out of the process personally, never wanting to show them to anyone else; indeed, never even re-reading them myself. My plan, if you could call it that, was to quietly fill another eighty-seven or so before I cark it, and for them to be thrown away when I do.

Which is still my plan – with one addition. I was suddenly struck with the burning desire to re-read all of them and select the best content for one Master Journal. For my kids after I died. A sort of personal 'Dad's loving advice from beyond the grave' self-help book.

The more I thought about it, the more the idea appealed. To get started I needed a journal of sufficient quality to honour the idea. After an afternoon online browsing, I found the perfect item. Eye-wateringly expensive, it cost more than all my other journals put together. But when it arrived, I knew it was worth every cent, from the beautiful green leather cover alone.

Carefully opening it, with one of Dad's leaky fountain pens I wrote 'CSTMTM' in the middle of the front page. It stands for 'Courageously Strive To Make The Most Of Your Life Whilst Having The Courage To Be Imperfect'. As good as any summary for the advice that I wanted to impart in the pages that followed.

The more eagle-eyed amongst you might have noticed the full acronym would actually be CSTMTMOYLWHTCTBI. I wasn't trying to name a Welsh town, though, so CSTMTM it was. Now to fill it.

My idea was to go through each of my journals in turn. Wading through the embarrassingly self-indulgent personal stuff about how I wanted to lose weight, or hated my boss etc, in a search for the more interesting timeless stuff. Nuggets of wisdom that might be useful for my kids as they made their way in the world. I might only get one quote that qualified from an entire journal. And that was fine. I was after quality, not quantity. I would then write these selected pieces into the Master Journal for posterity.

It was immensely enjoyable and enlightening. I didn't pressure myself on timing. Instead, I did it when the mood struck and the circumstances allowed. Over the first five years

I whiled away many a happy hour transcribing passages from all manner of sources. Quotes from Montaigne, 'Reflect on everything, regret nothing'; poems from Kipling, 'If you can dream and not make dreams your master . . .'; aphorisms from Nietzsche, 'Only thoughts which come from walking have value'; wisdom from Holocaust survivor Viktor Frankl, 'What man actually needs is not some tensionless state, but rather the striving and struggling for some goal worthy of him.'

At times as I was sitting in my damp under-garage study, writing in my stupidly expensive Master Journal with my dad's old leaky fountain pens, I felt a little like a seventh-century monk with a quill transcribing invaluable historical documents onto parchment in a castle tower for future generations.

There was so much wonderful stuff I had forgotten I had written down. Modern wisdom from LA jails, 'GABOS – Game Ain't Based On Sympathy'; the seven Ps acronym from my dad's naval career, 'PPPPPPP – Prior Preparation and Planning Prevents Piss-Poor Performance'; even my own musings, such as 'Everything in life is a choice – decide don't slide.'

And it wasn't all serious stuff either. I often found myself laughing out loud when I came across such passages as Albert Einstein's 'Two things are infinite, the universe and human stupidity. And I'm not sure about the universe.' Or the text my mate Andrew had sent me saying, 'I have sex daily! . . . no hold on I mean I have *dyslexia*.'

Taken individually none of the quotes might be that remarkable, but to me, as a whole, it felt varied, pithy, random, entertaining, thought provoking and above all life affirming. Precisely what I'd hoped it would be.

Five years in, having distilled the wisdom from over thirty of my journals, the Master Journal was almost half full.

And then I had a sudden change of heart. It was caused by the combination of the imminent twenty-first birthday of my younger son Harry and a conversation with a dear friend.

'The "voice from the grave" notion is a lovely idea,' she said, 'but wouldn't it be more use now, as they're starting out with their lives, rather than later after you die, when all their major life choices will probably have already been made?'

Put like that, it was hard to argue.

I got the journal professionally scanned and stored on my laptop. I then wrote a card for Harry explaining the idea behind the journal, and saying that the remaining blank pages were for him to fill with *his* wisdom and thoughts as he progressed through life's great adventure.

At the same time as I gave Harry the original hard copy on his birthday, I sent soft copies to Grace and Eve and Alex explaining that although Harry was getting the actual Master Journal, it had obviously been created for all of them and the scanned copies were, I hoped, equally thought provoking and entertaining, despite the lack of gilt edges.

And that was the end of it. Or so I thought.

Rather wonderfully, however, when people heard about the journal, they often asked to see it. Others asked if they could borrow it. So many people expressed an interest and responded positively that I eventually ended up in discussions with a publisher about taking it to a wider audience than just the original four intended.

It was a fascinating process. They said they could see huge potential in 'The Green Book', but had some suggestions. Unfortunately, to my mind, the changes they wanted to make would have made it less, not more, special. They wanted to order the quotes into sections like 'Work', 'Death' and 'Relationships', whereas I thought keeping the utter randomness of them was essential. Much to my horror, they also suggested presenting it in conventional type. I felt my messy handwriting and the different colour inks I had used were an important part of its charm, authenticity and difference.

After much debate, I came to realise the obvious truth that what made the Master Journal special was that I *hadn't* written it to get it published. And the moment I did, it would lose its charm. So I decided to stick with the original objective of four readers.

Truth be told, I fear not even hitting that target. I suspect, given their silence on the matter, that, wonderful though I passionately believe the journal to be, a number of my children might not share my opinion – and have joined Eve in mentally filing the book away in the 'River I Don't Give a Shit' category.

A prophet is never honoured in his own country and all that . . .

25

Queen Camel 4

I SOON DISCOVERED that revolting coffee was merely the first of a long list of challenges involved in living with Mum. For the first time in over thirty years, I had to sleep in a single bed. It shouldn't logically make a difference, but I found it played havoc with my ability to get even a half-decent night's kip.

And the food. Oh my God, the food. Forget the cancer and the dodgy heart, I'm surprised Mum's diet hadn't long since killed her. I like to think of myself as an extremely unfussy carefree eater, but the stream of heavily processed, sugar-packed, cheese-smothered microwaved crap was relentless. I started to crave vegetables. And I'm the man who constantly takes the piss out of Kate for all the expensive organic produce she buys. 'Dirty veg', as the kids and I call it. Now I'd happily have walked ten miles to a farmer's market to buy some, if circumstances allowed.

The physical challenges were the least of it, however. I loved my Mum to the moon and back, but fuck me sideways, she could be annoying. Maddeningly stubborn, irrational and confusing. The simple task of writing her shopping list before going to the shops would drive the Pope to drink.

'You've written strawberry jam here, Mum, but I can see you've got two unopened jars in the cupboard.'

'Yes dear, strawberry jam, please,' she'd reply.

'No, Mum, I know you've written strawberry jam on the list. I said you've got two full jars already.'

'Yes please, a jar of that nice Morrison's jam.'

'Mum, have you got your hearing aid on?'

'Of course, I've got my hearing aid on! What makes you ask that?'

'It's just I'm trying to explain I don't think we need any more strawberry jam. We already have two jars.'

'Yes, a jar of Morrison's strawberry jam.'

'Mum, I don't think you're hearing me properly. WE DON'T NEED MORE STRAWBERRY JAM. YOU'VE GOT TWO UNOPENED JARS OF THE MORRISON'S STRAWBERRY JAM YOU LIKE IN THE CUPBOARD.'

'I can hear you perfectly well, Nigel. And I'd like another jar of strawberry jam,' she tartly replied.

So I'd give in and buy the chuffing jam. And put it in the cupboard next to the other two jars. And that was merely the first item on her list.

'Mum, we've already got three litres of fresh milk in the fridge.'

'Yes, milk, please . . .'

You can guess the rest. I'd end up pouring two litres of sour milk down the sink a few days later.

And the list had thirty-odd items. Forget the Pope, I was seriously considering taking up drink before we got halfway down it.

But she was my mum and I loved her. And the point of this trip was to spend time with her. Proper time. Warts and all. Not nick off to London, when the going got tough or boring. The plan was to be present with her. Listen. Let her vent, be irrational, boss me about. Whatever she wanted.

The truth is that the good far outweighed the bad. We settled into a sort of glorious routine. We played Scrabble, did jigsaws, watched *Antiques Roadshow*, ate three meals a day together, and listened to BBC Radio 4 blaring incredibly loudly from her ancient kitchen transistor set, heating whacked up to sauna levels.

With the help of my friend Giles's young son, I downloaded Amazon Prime onto my iPad ('This is brilliant, Nigel, it's a *vintage* iPad!' he exclaimed when I handed it to him), so she could watch the films she read about in her daily newspaper. (Mum being one of those rare people who still got an actual physical copy of *The Times* every day.)

The film she most wanted to watch was *Fisherman's Friends*. For three reasons. First, because it is set in the West Country near where she grew up. Secondly, because both *The Times* and my brother had given it a good review. Thirdly, and most importantly, because one of the main stars in it was James Purefoy.

Mum was very excited that not only was Purefoy rumoured to be the next James Bond, taking over from Daniel Craig, but that *he was my friend*. He'd been my classmate at The Park School in Yeovil.

To listen to her describe it, we were inseparable bosom buddies, but truth be told I hadn't spoken to him in over fifty years and have absolutely no memory of him. I'm sure he doesn't of me either. I didn't want to burst Mum's 'We are watching *Nigel's friend's* film tonight' bubble, so kept my non-recollection to myself.

I set up Mum's sitting-room as a mini in-home cinema, arranging three seats in a row: Mum's armchair in the middle, with mine and her carer's either side. I then propped my tiny vintage iPad up on a coffee table in front of her. Finally, I made a big fuss of turning all the lights off, getting her a glass of Prosecco and two of the ginger biscuits she liked to set the mood.

It was obvious the screen was too small for her poor eyesight, and the sound not quite loud enough for failing hearing, but it made no difference. We sat there holding hands for two blissful hours – her pretending she could see and hear the film, me pretending I knew which actor James Purefoy was.

'Wasn't he good, Nidgey?' she asked as the film ended.

'Reckon his was the best performance in it, Mum,' I lied, as to this day I still don't know which of the fishermen James played.

And whatever the entertainment, I was constantly being surprised by out-of-date food.

'Nidgey, there's an open pack of roasted peanuts in the drawer under the fridge,' she said as we sat down to a game of Scrabble. 'Let's have some whilst playing.'

I poured them into a bowl and put a handful into my mouth. All the signs – Mum's comment, the clothes clip on the opened bag – had been that these were a recent purchase. But no, you had to be ever vigilant at 6 Mildmay Drive.

'Best Before November 2017,' I read on the pack, having spat the nuts into the kitchen bin. Over three years expired, but a marked improvement on the coffee.

We spent more time together than we ever had before. And it was a privilege and delight. She asked me to sit in on her doctor's visits. I drove her for her hospital appointments. We even managed to reach an accommodation of sorts on the weekly shopping lists (basically I just ended up buying everything on them without question).

When she took one of her daily naps, I'd walk around the local lanes and fields. My parents had bought a house here in 1976 and, apart from a couple of years when Dad worked in Switzerland, had lived in the village ever since.

Queen Camel is a small community with a population of less than a thousand. Mum and Dad moved twice within the village over their forty-five years' residence, so I got into the habit of doing a loop on my walks that passed all three of the houses of my childhood.

The first, 'Whitegates', which didn't actually have a white gate (or garden, much to the disappointment of my eight-year-old self); the second, 'Overton House', on the main road, whose windows always used to rattle when trucks sped past on the main road that splits the village in half; and now here, 6 Mildmay Drive, where Mum would be seeing out her last days.

I'd include the cobbled path and church on my route. The church is the village's most (let's be honest, only) notable landmark, as it boasts the heaviest set of six bells in the world. I've always wondered if that 'set of six' qualification makes the record meaningless. Does any other church even have a set of six? Or is it the standard number for church towers, and therefore Queen Camel is crushing it with a truly remarkable bell weight record? I've never wanted to properly investigate, in case six is indeed a ludicrously tiny sub-category and therefore rob my hometown of its crowning glory.

Dad is buried in the churchyard so I'd include a visit to his grave to say hello and a prayer. When the leaves are off the trees Mum can see his headstone from her bedroom. I'm not sure if that is lovely or sad, but it is what it is.

I'm a sucker for small ancient English churches and feel that the thousands of them scattered throughout the countryside, taken as a whole, are one of the great wonders of the world. So if the weather allowed, I'd extend my loop and stroll across the fields to the next village – Weston Bampfylde – as it contained my all-time favourite small church. (It's pushed hard by the simply sensational St Aldhelm's Chapel in Dorset, but that's for another time. Let me just say that if you ever get the chance to visit it, I guarantee you won't be disappointed. Google it.)

I say village, but Weston Bampfylde is so small it's officially defined as a hamlet. Since records began, and its entry in the 1086 Domesday Book, the population has never been over fifty. And yet it has the most glorious church – built in approximately 1217.

That date is so old it can be hard to get your head properly around it. Not by Aboriginal standards, of course, but consider, as a contrast, the oldest church in Australia. It's on the banks of the Hawkesbury River in New South Wales in the small settlement of Ebenezer. It's gorgeous and I highly recommend a visit. But despite being the oldest in the country, it is still a full *600* years younger than the one in Weston Bampfylde.

And here's the thing. Even though it's a Grade II listed building and designated as a World Heritage Site, it is still simply a regular working community church. There are no signs to it or shop or tourists. It is understated to the point of invisibility. 'Holy Cross is a small church with a big heart,' it charmingly says in its leaflet.

It holds weekly services – as it's been doing regularly for the past 800 years. And amazingly, you can visit any day of the year as they keep it unlocked and open for all comers. To marvel at the history contained within ('old' most definitely having positive connotations in this case), enjoy the simple pared-back beauty, say a prayer, or simply sit in the peace and quiet and gather your thoughts and count your blessings. I've been doing exactly that for years.

On my last walk I picked up the visitors book and had a flick through. There, on the very first page, I saw I had made an entry. On 21 August 2003 – the week I flew over from Australia because Dad had been committed to hospital and was being moved to a home.

Further on, I saw another entry on 15 December 2014, the week I came over for Dad's funeral. I'm sure if the earlier books were available for viewing I'd find many more entries marking other significant milestones in my life. And here I was again – this time saying a prayer for my mum, not my dad. I made another entry in the book and walked back over the fields.

26

Bronte Biathlon

I HAD MY birthday whilst I was staying with Mum. It was a very low-key affair. When I woke up I saw an old postcard had been slipped under my door in the night. On the back of it, in semi-legible scrawly handwriting, was the message: 'The best I can do in the circumstances! Much love Mum xxxx.' It was incredibly sweet as she had gone to bed before me the evening before, and must have got up in the middle of the night to put it there. Given her extremely poor and painful mobility, it must have taken a huge effort to get out of bed, shuffle to my room with her stability frame, and then bend down at the door. God love her.

In the evening, my long-standing friend from university, Giles, was coming with his son for a birthday dinner in the village pub with my brother, his wife and me, but beyond that it would be a quiet day sitting at home with Mum – like all the others. If you'd asked me three months earlier how I thought I'd be spending my birthday, I would have confidently informed you, 'Doing the Bronte Biathlon and then having a relaxed dinner at home with my wife and kids in.' Funny old life.

Because of the time difference, when I got up in Queen Camel it had already been my birthday in Australia for a full twenty hours, so my phone was packed with lovely messages from family and friends back home. Some sent pictures, other videos, all serving to bring the contrast between Sydney and Queen Camel into sharp relief.

Australia was in the middle of summer so the pictures were of people smiling, thumbs up on the beach, under clear blue skies. England, of course, was in the depths of winter, dealing with the challenges presented by the back-to-back storms Ciara, then Dennis. There were over 500 flood warnings across the country, standing water in the fields around Mum's house, and the skies were permanently overcast – apart from when they took a break to hurl rain in downpours of biblical proportions.

It was so bad I couldn't resist taking the piss when Kate raised the weather during a call.

'The weather sounds awful,' she said. 'It even made the news here.'

'Ah, it's not been too bad – it's only rained twice.'

'Really?' she replied.

'Yep, once for the whole of February and then again for the whole of March.'

And it got dark so stupidly early. Mum and I were turning our houselights on at 4.15 pm, whereas in Sydney people were still larking about outside in broad daylight at 8.30 in the evening. God, I missed home: my family, my friends, the light, the dog, my house, the lack of mud.

And Bronte – the ocean. Which brings me to the Bronte Biathlon. When in Sydney, I do it every Wednesday evening and it's become one of the absolute favourite parts of my summer routine. With my birthday falling on a Wednesday, if I hadn't made this trip to see Mum, I would currently have been warming up on the Bronte beach promenade with the other athletes.

I say 'athletes', as that is indeed what the other partici-pants are. Lithe, supple and dressed in skimpy figure-hugging lycra, they whizz along through the course in as little as twenty minutes. I, on the other hand, am what you could call an anomaly. Wearing baggy old rugby shorts and an oversized 'Sydney Skinny Event Crew' T-shirt, I rarely complete the course in less than forty minutes. But I adore it, irrespective of often breasting the finish line well after some of the front runners have had a celebratory beer and left for home.

Thanks to the late summer evenings, the races start at 6.30 pm and follow a course along the coast path, through Waverley cemetery to Clovelly, where you jump in the ocean, do a 200-metre swim, run the beach barefoot, do another 200-metre swim, then run back along the cliffs to Bronte. Every step and every stroke heaven.

No two events are the same. The tide can be out, meaning there's so little water in Clovelly Bay you can't dive in, and have to be careful not to scrape yourself on the rocks as you swim. Other weeks, the tide is high and the weather so rough it feels like you're in a giant outdoor washing machine. And it's always beautiful whatever the conditions – it being a rare week when you don't spot at least one interesting piece of sea life on your way to the beach and back. (If only I was an underwater photographer . . .)

The running portion is equally rewarding, with stunning views across the ocean to Bondi in the north and the national park at Maroubra in the south. And importantly – for me, anyway – the cemetery adds a very special element to proceedings. Jogging past all those graves, containing the remains of thousands of people long gone, who all once had their own dreams and fears, triumphs and disasters, love affairs and heartbreak, regrets and contentment, serves as a huge outdoor memento mori. It provides a useful weekly reminder to count my blessings and make the most of my life before it's my time to join them underground.

Given all the above, I don't really want to go any faster. (This is not a lame excuse for my unfitness.) The longer I take, the longer I get to enjoy it. I'm not denying I wouldn't enjoy losing a bit of weight and my relaxed jogging pace isn't hugely conducive to that. But for me the point of life generally has never been about trying to go ever faster. And, specifically, not on my Wednesday evenings.

Whilst I suspect the leader of the event – the unfeasibly fit and handsome Troy – thinks I'm mad, he also knows I serve a useful marketing purpose in successfully broadening his recruitment drive.

'I'm not very fit and have never done a biathlon before,' I heard a worried man ask him one Wednesday. 'Do you think I could do it?'

'Of course,' I heard him reply. '*Nigel* does it!'

On another occasion I was a little late, arriving only minutes before 6.30 pm. The moment I approached the signing-in desk, a nervous woman was hurriedly ushered over to me as Troy's relieved cry rang out, 'Excellent – here he is! I told you he was coming. I'll introduce you now. He'll stay with you until you want to pull ahead. Don't worry – you're guaranteed to never come last in the Bronte Biathlon.'

Happy to be of service.

Given this philosophy, it was a lovely surprise when I struck up a relationship with Carl Honoré, the author of *In Praise of Slow* and the face of the growing global slow movement. We shared a speaking platform in Slovenia and ever since have remained in contact. It's enormously comforting to learn from his work that the views reflected in my approach to the Bronte Biathlon are apparently gaining in popularity and there are legions of people around the world increasingly focusing on the quality of their experiences and contribution – rather than speed – in their third trimester.

27

Singing for my supper

I'VE LOST COUNT of the number of speaking engagements I've done. I'm confident it is comfortably over 500. I love doing them, but it isn't the occasions that have gone smoothly that stick in the memory. It's the clusterfucks. The gigs that to this day make me feel like that bloke in Edvard Munch's *Scream* when I think of them. Whilst I can't remember even half of the gigs I've done that went well, I can vividly recall *every single* one that didn't.

Most of them have been my fault, some of them not. An early example of the latter almost put me off public speaking altogether, before I'd even got properly started. I'd been hired to deliver a keynote in Perth about creativity in advertising, and give my opinion about what makes a good ad and what doesn't.

It's a subject close to my heart. I spent a thoroughly enjoyable fortnight preparing by compiling a showreel of ten classic ads. Each one was carefully chosen for an important point I wanted to make about creativity.

With such a wonderful selection of videos to show, the speech wrote itself. Ten minutes to play the actual ads; three or four minutes of explanation from me after each about the point I felt they illustrated; then ten minutes for Q&A. Bingo. That's your hour keynote right there. I was comfortable, confident and enormously looking forward to it.

On the day I was met in the venue by a rather stressed marketing manager. 'Hello, Nigel. I'm Paul, we spoke on the phone. Thank you for coming all this way. We're having a spot of trouble with the technology, I'm afraid.'

'No worries,' I told him. 'I'm sure we can sort it out in the AV run-through. I'm very low maintenance as I haven't got any slides to present off – just ten TV ads on a memory stick.

'That's the problem. The AV isn't working.'

'At all?'

'Well, we've managed to project images on the screen, but we just can't get the sound to work.'

And he was right. They couldn't.

So . . . I had to give an hour's speech entirely based around ten silent ads, none of which made any sense without their soundtrack. Munch's man had nothing on me as I walked off stage forty minutes later. The horror. Oh, the horror.

On another occasion I was asked to present to the sales force of a Canadian bank – in Cancun, Mexico, of all places. My slot was after dinner. Well, I was *told* it was going to be after dinner. It turned out it was during dinner.

I presented on a raised stage, set back from a room of thirty or so round tables. Each was populated by eight drunk, French-speaking bank employees, none of whom – even the ones who could actually speak English – gave a fish's tit about 'The characteristics of effective business leadership'.

This was clearly more of a holiday for them than a serious conference and they were too busy letting their hair down and getting stuck into the tasty chicken curry, noisily being served around them, to pay any attention to the bloke on stage at the far end of the room. And, unfortunately, the fact that the AV actually worked on this occasion was of bugger all use to me as, for this speech, I didn't have any videos.

I naively thought Mexico would be the nadir. Wrong. Very wrong. Barely a year later, I was flown to Fiji to do the closing keynote speech at a car dealership conference.

The briefing for this engagement was very specific. The audience would be made up entirely of young ambitious male car salesmen. The brief was: 'Be heavy on the entertainment, light on the serious stuff.' During the phone briefing, the client was even more directional.

'It's a rowdy, demanding group,' he told me. 'In previous years, the acts who've done best at this conference have been the more . . . shall we say, risqué ones. I've read your books and the stuff about sex, for example, would go over well. That story about your mate caught wanking by his wife and her client – it's the type of thing they would love.'

'Really?' I said, slightly intrigued by the use of the word 'acts' as opposed to 'speakers'.

'Yeah, and that time your daughter said to the kindergarten gym teacher, "We don't touch Daddy's willy, because it's dirty."

Classic. That's the tone we're after. Blue is fine. Non-PC is fine. The more shocking the better, frankly. They're easily bored and your act' – *that word again* – 'is coming at the end of the conference. They'll be after a laugh, not a business sermon,' he rather unnecessarily summarised.

Rightio.

It wasn't a bad brief, to be honest. I'd often been asked before a conference to tone things down, but never to tone things *up*.

I took the direction to heart and wrote the bluest, rudest, most potentially offensive – and hopefully funny – speech I ever had. Standing at the back of the stage waiting to go on, I felt more like Lenny Bruce than Simon Sinek.

As the MC began my introduction, I felt a hand on my shoulder. It was Jeet, the local conference event organiser, not my client.

'Hi Jeet,' I turned and whispered. 'How can I help?'

'I have a favour, Mr Nigel. Please don't go on stage straight away after he has finished introducing you.'

'Err . . . right.'

'Just a two-minute delay, Mr Nigel. Very important.'

'Okay . . . what for?'

'Special surprise. To honour our conference guests this past week, we are going to get a choir – the Fijian Christian Children's Choir – to sing the Australian national anthem after your speech.'

'*After* my speech? Good.'

'Yes, but before your speech we are going to seat the choir on the floor between the stage and the front row, so they are ready to perform immediately after you finish. It will only take a couple of minutes.'

And to my horror, that's what he did. Ushering forty or so angelic ten and eleven-year-olds – all dressed in immaculate uniform; innocent, trusting, Christian boys and girls – into the room to obediently sit down cross-legged in front of the stage and eagerly stare up at me.

Marvellous. As I hurriedly rifled through my speech notes, searching in vain for at least one story that was remotely appropriate for this new – wildly off-brief – audience I found myself wishing I was in Mexico . . .

But it's the disastrous gigs that were *my* fault that are the most painful to remember. The others can be turned into amusing war stories where I don't shoulder the blame. One such occasion was a gig in the Midwest of America ten or so years ago. It was going well, but fifteen or so minutes in, I became increasingly aware of a man in the front row who clearly looked unhappy – terrible body language, crossed arms, scowl on his face, and staring directly at me the whole time.

I take my speaking work seriously, genuinely wanting to connect with my audience. And this bloke clearly had a problem. I wanted to help him if I could. Perhaps he wanted to ask a question? Or challenge me on one of my points? I'd be fine with either.

I paused mid-presentation and, with a smile, said to him, 'Excuse me, sir, I couldn't help noticing you seem like you might have something to ask? No need to wait until the end. Feel free to fire away now.'

'It's not a question.' he replied, staring coldly at me, 'it's a statement. Your language has really upset my wife.'

'Ah, okay, sir, I see. My sincere apologies.' I turned to the woman sat next to him. 'And to you, madam. I'll make sure you'll be hearing no more bad language this afternoon.'

I then carried on and finished the rest of my keynote as normal. Well, it might have seemed normal on the outside. But on the inside, I was crushed. Soul-flatteningly crushed. Because he had made a perfectly valid point.

The punchline to one of my early stories had, indeed, revolved around the 'f word'. What the hell was I thinking saying 'fuck' in the Midwest? An area famous for the politeness and well-spoken good manners of its population. If one person had felt moved to speak up about it, how many more in the audience had I offended who hadn't said anything? And it was such a needless mistake, as I could have easily chosen a number of equally effective warm-up stories that involved no bad language. But I'd been thoughtless and careless. My intention had been pure, but as I often tell my kids it's positive impact that matters, not merely good intentions. And I'd fucked up. Excuse the language.

It still bothers me to this day.

But my all-time worst memory is of a gig I did in Shanghai. The speech itself went okay. No thunderous applause or standing ovation, but alright. It wasn't my performance that made me feel awful – it was the one straight after me. It was given by a bloke called Fredrik Haren. He slayed the audience, had them laughing and clapping throughout, and ended to a tremendous ovation. His content was no better than mine, yet I had flatlined and he had killed it. And the reason was painfully, painfully obvious.

Haren had peppered his speech throughout with *local* references. He had taken the time and trouble to illustrate his points and stories using local names, locations and characteristics. He mentioned walking along the beautiful Bund promenade, getting caught in the horrendous Hongqiao traffic and told an excellent joke revolving around the Shanghainese's reputation for arrogance. He talked about recent Chinese films and politics. Even cracked out a couple of phrases in Mandarin.

I, on the other hand, gave them my usual stuff. With passion and commitment – but my normal stuff. Now, in my defence, up until that point in my speaking career, all my audiences had been 'Anglo-Western'. Even if I was talking in Mexico or Fiji, it had still been to an Australian or Canadian audience. The Shanghai gig was my first to a properly 'non-Western' audience. And I had waltzed in there with unwitting – but shameful nevertheless – arrogance and assumed one size fits all. I'm wincing now as I remember.

Simply. Not. Good. Enough. Amateur night at the open mic spot. However you want to describe it, I was schooled by Haren that day.

Painful and humbling though it is to recall, I'm grateful for this 'learning opportunity' as the Americans call it. You learn best from your own mistakes, after all. It's an education I took to heart and have never forgotten: *you have to not only honour the opportunity, but also the audience.* And that means in each case putting in some genuine effort to get to know their specific circumstances, and making it clear to them that you have done so.

There are also profound lessons from the disastrous gigs that weren't my fault – and they're more important and broadly applicable than simply watching your language or being sure to pay appropriate respect to local nuances. Gigs like the ones in Fiji, Mexico and Perth went wrong for reasons completely beyond my control. I couldn't have predicted the appearance of the children's choir, or stopped the drunk Canadians from loudly tucking into their chicken curry, or miraculously made the AV work in Perth.

And that's a good metaphor for life generally. You never know what's around the corner. You can't determine the cards you are going to be dealt (the bad news the doctor unexpectedly tells you, the global economy crushing your business, the shark sighting the morning you're due to put on a community ocean race you've sold 2000 tickets to); only how you play those cards. And we always have a choice. We can focus on the injustice and horror of the moment and despair. Or acknowledge the reality of the situation and single-mindedly focus on how to make the best of it. I'm not saying it makes everything peachy, but I am saying it is the better choice.

Did this attitude make the above three gigs a success? Hell, no – they were still pride-crushing torture. But I made the best of them, and in each case know that my efforts helped the situation, not made it worse.

There's an apocryphal story about a Zen Buddhist that, despite its dubious origins, I feel contains a relevant insight here. The Zen master asks his student, 'If you are carrying a mug of coffee and someone bumps into you and you spill the coffee, who is to blame for the coffee on the ground?'

'Obviously the person who bumped into you,' replies the student.

'Not so. If you had filled the mug with tea, the ground would have tea on it not coffee.'

The point being that if you fill your mug with a 'calm, humorously resigned, make the best of things' attitude, then when life metaphorically bumps into you, it's more likely *that* is what will spill out – not self-pity or despair. It's easier said than done, I know; but something I strive for all the same.

28

Memory Lane 2

THE GREENWELL POINT family weekend might have been full of powerful triggers for intense visits down Memory Lane, but Mum's house took it to another level. Not just the house itself – the pictures in it. Framed pictures hanging on all the walls and covering every surface. They were *everywhere*. Inescapable.

They lovingly chronicled each life stage and family milestone. Weddings, christenings, Christmas holidays, funerals, university degree ceremonies, first steps, military passing-out parades, Dad on the bridge of a ship during a tour of command, Dad in uniform at Buckingham Palace, my brother and I at Mum's eightieth birthday.

In the room where I wrote this there was a large wooden frame on the windowsill. The photo in it reminded me of a number of the holiday snaps Kate and I have framed from our holidays as a young family. This one was of my mum, dad, brother and me fifty years ago, standing waist deep in beautifully blue water under a bright sunny sky. We all have our arms around each other and are beaming broadly. Both my brother and I have strikingly blond hair. Dad is in red boardshorts, Mum in a flatteringly patterned and cut one-piece. In the top-left hand corner of the picture, someone (probably Mum, given the indescribably awful handwriting) has written in large letters: 'Easter holiday 1973. In the Gulf of Mexico. Ole!'

Looking at it brought a lump to my throat and made me want to rush into the room next door, where Mum had fallen asleep again in her chair, and give her a huge hug. She wasn't always an immobile, anxious old lady. She was once youthful, energetic and carefree – in love and on holiday in a foreign land, with her dashing Navy captain husband and their two young sons.

In addition to the framed photos, Mum long had a tradition of sticking photographs with Blu-tac on her wooden kitchen cupboard doors. Hundreds of them, from top to bottom, covering every inch, so you could no longer see the wood only the metal handles poking out from amongst them.

But while the entire house might have been full of pictures, her kitchen was the real nave of the church. It was a shrine to the extended family, with every family member represented – from grandkids in Leeds and Sydney to cousins in Toronto and Kelowna.

Whenever I showed her a photo she liked, she always said, 'Oh, that's lovely, Nidgey, can I have a copy printed out, please?' And up it went.

Over the years, as space for ever more photos had become increasingly difficult to find, Kate and I hit on the brilliant idea of sending Mum one of those digital picture frames that can show hundreds of different photos in turn on a permanent loop.

Well, *we* thought it was a brilliant idea. Mum hated it. Never turned it on. When we visited and saw she hadn't even got it on display, we thought it was because she didn't know how to use it. We checked we had correctly loaded it with a bunch of her recent favourite photos and turned it on for her.

Next morning, we came downstairs to find she had switched it to static so it only showed one photo. We explained it was cleverly designed to show all the photos in turn and switched it back to 'revolve'. The following morning we saw she had taken it down completely and put it away somewhere.

However, the biggest memory jolt on this trip wasn't from the pictures in the house. It was from a news article . . .

29

Sherborne Prep

THE ARTICLE WAS printed off from the Somerset Live news website, dated 1 October 2019. It caught my eye when picking up a pile of paper I'd knocked off the side table next to Mum's desk. 'Fixated paedophile headmaster told nursing staff to have sex with him!' screamed the headline.

The story was depressingly sad. As often happens in these cases, a man suffering from dementia in an old people's home had lost his inhibitions, and his conversation was made up almost entirely of sexually explicit comments. An Independent Inquiry into Child Abuse Report had just been published. In it was a remark from a dementia nurse caring for this man that he'd said to her, 'Come here and let me fuck you, like I fucked the little boys at my school.'

The school was Sherborne Prep. My school. And Robin Lindsay, the headmaster. My headmaster. Not all trips down Memory Lane are as pleasant as the Gulf of Mexico.

I happen to believe we diminish ourselves when we whip a man on his way to hell, so I'll refrain from venting my personal feelings about 'Mr Robin', as we were made to call him. Instead, I'll stick to the facts.

Robin Lindsay was headmaster of Sherborne Prep from 1953 to 1998. Official concerns were raised about his behaviour on many occasions, the first as early as 1974. Yet his behaviour continued unimpeded for another twenty-four years.

He was the classic predatory paedophile, who would groom both the boys and the parents. His chosen target was always the boarders, never the day boys. The boarders lived in a building within the school grounds, Netherton House. And where did Mr Robin choose to locate his bedroom? Yep, right in the middle of us in Netherton House.

How is it possible this went on for so long? That it took until 1998 for him to be forced out and banned from any further roles involving children?

It's complex. After decades thinking about it, I reckon there were four major reasons behind the catastrophic failure of care.

The first is straight-up classic denial. As a loving parent it was just so appallingly, unthinkably awful to believe, for one moment, that you had sent your young son into the sole care of an abuser that you simply *didn't* believe it. When little Jimmy hesitantly expressed reservations to Mummy and Daddy about some of Mr Robin's more strange behaviour, it was brushed off as either your exaggeration or his eccentricity. Sexual abuse was simply not an option to be entertained.

The second is initially hard to believe. According to the district commissioner of Somerset police who conducted one of the official inquiries, some of the parents *simply didn't want to make a fuss*. Many were families living in borderline poverty. Lindsay had given them a deal so they could afford to send their offspring to a 'good' school and thereby give them opportunities they themselves had never had. If your son was passing his exams and not suicidal, why make a fuss about a little bit of *claimed* dodgy shower-room shenanigans, and potentially jeopardise his entire educational gateway to a better life?

The third is that Lindsay was sensationally adept at grooming the parents. Most of them thought he was fantastic. He carefully polished his image as an eccentric educational genius – one who, left to his own devices, could get your son into one of the good schools that otherwise the child wouldn't have the opportunity to attend.

He had lots of evidence to point to. Hundreds of Sherborne Prep boys had gone on to Sherborne High School – a genuinely good school. But one, in fact, that had nothing to do with the Prep school. Lindsay just very effectively made it seem as if it was the natural feeder school. A bit like Jim Jones in Jonestown, you simply had to trust him and everything would be alright. Ironically, and excuse the pun, it was of bugger-all use to me as we couldn't afford to go to the High School anyway.

Which leads on to the fourth reason. It's just so damn difficult to be sure. Obviously, if he had been caught on camera sexually abusing hundreds of young boys, he would have been locked up quick as you like. But things are rarely that easy and clear-cut.

For a start the primary witnesses were young boys – isolated, far away from home and any loved ones. Mr Robin was the ultimate, and only, authority figure in their lives. Was it really wrong that Mr Robin took you to his study alone, and told you to take your shorts and pants off, before bending you over his knees to spank you with his bare hand, because you hadn't finished all your vegetables at dinnertime? How the hell would I know at such a tender age?

Was it normal or weird that he would regularly get a chair and place it in front of the showers after rugby games and tell you to turn around and wash between your buttocks? The answer now, nearing sixty, is obvious.

Why didn't the other teachers do something? Again, I genuinely think they didn't *know*. One did heroically resign because of his suspicions – take a bow, Mr Llewellyn – but they were suspicions, not proof.

And whilst Mr Robin might be fiddling with you, you didn't know what he was doing with anyone else. Or if he even *was* doing anything with anyone else. I truly believe – choose to believe – that no-one knew the true extent of his behaviour.

At the time I certainly didn't. And to this day many *still* don't believe the seemingly unarguable evidence. At his farewell event after he was finally driven out of the school, 700 people raucously sang 'For he's a jolly good fellow' to him as he departed.

I only ever raised it with my Dad once. I was nine at the time. It was a short conversation.

'Dad, there are rumours that Mr Robin is interfering with some of the boys,' I nervously ventured.

'Ha, what's wrong with *my* son that he's never chosen him!' he joked, whilst affectionately ruffling my hair.

In the face of this almost perfect combination of instinctive denial and lack of deeper curiosity, I dropped the subject.

In later years, my attitude was that it was too late to raise it with my mum. I've always advised my kids to consider both their intention and, importantly, the actual likely outcome before they open their mouths. What would mine have been, in this specific situation, if I'd discussed it with Mum? To make her feel bad? To throw myself a pity party?

So like with my little James Purefoy secret, and in the classic tradition of buttoned-up, emotionally repressed Englishmen, it was something that I left undiscussed.

Regardless of talking with Mum, it's obviously something I've had to deal with personally. For better or worse, my philosophy regarding my prep school experience has been the same for fifty years and, indeed, has become how I deal with other things in my life.

The best way to describe my approach is taking the example of a rugby team going into the changing rooms at half-time, losing 25–0. Clearly, there's nothing they can do to change the score before they retake the field. Whatever they do – cry at the humiliation, criticise the ref, blame the full moon – it's 100 per cent guaranteed that the score will still be 25–0 when they jog back onto the pitch.

There is, however, everything they can do about changing the score by the end of the second half. So why pour your energy (emotional and otherwise) into trying to change things you can't, when instead you might pour your energy into those you can?

Reading that back just now, though, its simplicity makes me think that, maybe in my sixties, it mightn't hurt if one day I did actually arrange a chat with a qualified therapist, after all.

30

Leadershit

Because of my conference speaking, MC-ing and consulting work, I'm regularly exposed to the ever-evolving language of Management Speak. One year your thinking has to be 'blue sky'; the next 'joined up'. A few years ago you might 'reach out to people'; now you suggest 'touching base offline'.

As I approach sixty, it has become a huge source of secret pleasure studying it, and noticing the seemingly collectively agreed nanosecond that a phrase goes out of fashion. Instantly, no-one is 'squaring the circle' anymore as everyone is 'aligning the verticals'. I find myself quietly playing bullshit bingo – waiting excitedly in a meeting for someone to say 'rightsizing', or trying hard not to scream 'Yes!' and do a double fist-pump when someone else hits the jackpot, declaring she can't work on a new project as she 'hasn't got enough bandwidth'.

I also delight in hearing a hilarious phrase for the first time.

'Hello, Nigel, thanks so much for coming in at short notice,' a senior telecoms executive said to me recently as he strode into the boardroom. 'I have to warn you that we'll need to wrap up at 5.30 pm as I've got a hard end.'

'Beg your pardon, Stephen. You've got a what?'

'A hard end. I *have* to leave at 5.30.'

Call me the owner of a smutty mind, but I'm not sure that one is going to catch on.

But I get it. I understand businesses and companies down the passage of time have always had their own rhythms and rituals. That sometimes people feel the need to sound clever when under pressure to impress, or bluff when they're out of their depth, or use a euphemism for an unpleasant topic, or simply copy the latest jargon in a bid to fit in. And in all these cases, silly though it might sound, management speak has an understandable role to play.

It's the management books I find harder to put up with. Again, I understand the desire of business people to improve their performance by educating themselves. How executives are eager for lessons from all walks of life that might help them better succeed. And subsequently are interested in the wisdom of effective, sporting or wealthy people. Titles such as *The 7 Habits of Highly Effective People, How Champions Think* and *Wealth Secrets of the 1%* tap into this market.

Despite my reservations about some of the gobbledegook, platitudes and victor's wisdom contained within, good luck to the authors, I say. They're serving a purpose of sorts and meeting a need. Amongst the bollocksy phrases and waffle, they often do signpost a sensible point. Even common sense sometimes needs to be repackaged for a different time and a different market.

But where do you draw the line? Because, alongside the above books, you can also buy *Mob Rules: what the Mafia can teach the legitimate businessman*, or *Marketing Lessons from the Grateful Dead* or – and I'm not making this up – *The Psychopath's Guide to Success*.

Business lessons from gangsters, rock bands and psychopaths? But people lap it up. Particularly in America. I'm not saying H. L. Mencken was correct when he said, 'Nobody ever went broke underestimating the intelligence of the American people,' but I do feel business readers around the world have somehow crossed a rubicon where they'll read any old shit written by anyone.

And that's where Leadershit™ comes in.

I can't take any credit for the idea – it's the brainchild of my friend Chris. Chris had a long career as the successful CEO of a large multinational company, with the highly respected *Harvard Business Review* including him in their annual list of the world's top 100 CEOs at the end of his tenure.

Chris' idea is for us – well, mainly *me*, the lazy bastard – to write a management book called *The Lessons of Leadershit*. The front cover would have the word 'leadership' in the title with the 'p' crossed out and a 't' written in above it. No overestimating going on here.

Inside would be ten or so chapters. All of them written completely deadpan. There would be absolutely no joking or piss-taking (despite the lavatorial theme). A bit like the TV show *The Office*, the idea doesn't work if you don't wholeheartedly commit to it.

Each chapter would take a different aspect of the fine art of defecation and deconstruct it to pull out a business lesson. For example, Chapter 1 could be 'The Importance of

Being Prepared'. In it, I might write about how, while it's certainly important to make sure your supply chain is tested and fully operational before a major product launch, it's no less important – in many ways, much more – to ensure your lavatory holder has an ample supply of sheets (200 minimum; don't settle for less) before committing one's cheeks to the seat.

Chapter 2 might be 'Persistence': drawing the analogy between those times in business when declaring victory too soon is the cause of failure, and that moment on the throne when you think you might be finished bombing the porcelain sea, but stay sitting and actually manage to successfully squeeze that last one out.

Chapter 3 could be 'Priorities'. In business, of course, it's vitally important to stay focused – the main thing being to keep the main thing the main thing. Again, there's a useful porcelain parallel. You know, those rare occasions when a solitary drop of water flies up from the bowl and doesn't hit your leg or buttock, but instead *shoots precisely up your date*? And you think, 'Blimey, I wasn't expecting that and how does that even happen?' Soon, you're lost in thought, contemplating the flight path of the drop, the complex mechanics and coordinates that must have been in place for this freak event to occur. Before long, you don't know what day of the week it is. You can barely remember your own name. *Stay focused.*

And so on.

I reckon Chris is right and it could sell. And if it did, we'd have the unarguable proof that the world of management books has indeed jumped the shark – and we could all stop buying the bloody things.

31

INPOS

I'VE WRITTEN ABOUT my slightly embarrassing obsession with dates, and the patterns they make, in a previous book. I'm actually glad I owned up to it, as ever since I've regularly received emails and messages on social media, alerting me to particular dates that they think I might like.

These are from people I've never met who are just being supportive and friendly. It might be 'just noticed it's 19.09.19, thought of you' with a smiley emoji, or '20.02.20 today enjoy, Nige' with a thumbs-up emoji, or '12.1.21 palindrometastic!' 'Twosday' was a particular highlight – shout out to the kindred spirit who messaged me at 2.22 am on 22.2.2022. Call me an old softy but I really like getting them. It doesn't do any harm – and suggests, to me anyway, that maybe deep down humans are actually quite nice.

What I've never confessed to before, however, is my secret obsession with acronyms. The type I used in the Master Journal.

The slightly weird truth is they play a more important role in my life than simply being an entertaining hobby. For years, I've made up my own acronyms. And then used them on a daily basis. I thought it was just me until recently a friend of mine told me he signs all his emails and messages to his wife with EOIAFM.

I've never shown mine to anyone else. I write them on pads at the start of important meetings, have had them engraved on pens and watches, and mark them on my arm before big speeches. It's an entirely private thing. And if anyone else were to spot them, they would be utterly meaningless. A by no means comprehensive selection being: INPDS, CSTMTM, DG&ED, MM>MM, TB, DSTSS, HTAI, 6TTDT, API, LFEP&S, DI&ABT&LT, FFF.

Gobbledegook – and although you might be able to guess the last one, and I've already explained CSTMTM, the others are just a random collection of letters to anyone but me.

I use them to help me stay on track and strive to be the best man I can be and make the most of every day. Corny, I know – and I suspect that this confession will evoke fewer messages of support than my dates one – but for what it's worth, the key to the codes is as follows:

If Not Perfect Do Something
Courageously Strive To Make The Most
Delay Gratification and Endure Discomfort
Mindless Margins into Mindful Margins
Think Big

Don't Sweat The Small Stuff
Helpful Thoughts, Actions, Influences
Six Things To Do Today
Assume Positive Intent
Learn From Every Person and Situation
Don't Inflame and Amplify, Buy Time and Lower the
   Temperature

And, drum roll . . .

Fat, Forty and Fired

And there's me claiming I don't like self-help.

So, what does my friend's acronym stand for? EOIAFM. Every One Is A Fucking Moron. Slightly less self-helpy than mine, but a useful daily reminder, nevertheless, I suppose.

32

Starting over

THE TIME CAME for me to leave Queen Camel. Mum was still very ill, but it simply wasn't practical for me to stay in the UK any longer. My family, and life, was in Australia and a month was a long time away. I didn't want them to start getting used to not having me around.

Having said that, there was evidence some of them hadn't noticed I'd even gone in the first place. In my last week, as I was starting to pack up I noticed a little red dot on my iPhone, notifying me that '440 not 420' – one of my children – had sent me a message on the family Messenger group that I so loved. 'That's sweet,' I thought, 'he's sending me a "Have a nice flight, looking forward to seeing you soon" note.' I opened the app to read: 'Dad can you give me a lift from

Bondi Junction? It's chucking it down and I've just missed the bus.' Marvellous.

Aside from making sure that those family members who *had* noticed I was away didn't forget me, there was another deeply serious reason I had to return. Not to put too fine a point on it, I had to earn some money. Being in the West Country of England meant I had had to forego doing any public speaking. No speeches meant no income. And, unlike a number of our more well-heeled neighbours, no income was not a sustainable situation for the residents of The Burrow.

I was keen to hit the ground running on my return to make up for lost time – and earnings. Encouragingly, I had taken a number of bookings for later in the year whilst in Queen Camel. Most notably to MC the tour of a chap called Simon Sinek on his upcoming tour of Australia.

I was particularly pleased with this booking. Simon is a big deal in the corporate world. Amongst his many other notable achievements, he gave a TED speech that is the third-most watched of all time. Not just amongst business speeches – of all time on any subject. He has legions of fans and followers to go along with an incredibly high profile.

Doing the tour with him would be the perfect way to get back on the horse and let people know I was working again and available for bookings myself. The other reason I was pleased is because, unusually for me when it comes to the vast cesspit of business commentators out there, Simon was someone I genuinely admired. I've found his books insightful, enjoyable and actually *helpful* in a real-world context. So, all in all, it promised to be the perfect soft landing at Sydney airport to what would otherwise have been a rather scary financial predicament.

I busied myself planning a few surprises for Mum for soon after my departure. I wrote and sent a card to her, so it would arrive in the post on the first morning I wasn't there. I went through the pictures I had taken of us together whilst I'd been in the UK and sent one to a company to turn it into a jigsaw. Again, I arranged for it to be delivered in the week after my return home. It would be both a nice reminder of our time together and keep her entertained during the long days stuck inside, battling her various ailments.

So, despite the obvious sadness of leaving my mum, and all the unavoidable thoughts of 'Will I ever see her again?' – and guilt at living so stupidly far away – it would be fair to say I was full of enthusiasm and optimism for the future as I got on Qantas QF1 bound for Sydney and a world, unbeknownst to me, soon to be completely shut down by Covid-19.

33

Lockdown

WITHIN DAYS OF my arrival in Sydney, all my plans for an energetic burst of heroic business activity to get the family finances back on track were comprehensively blown out of the water. Forget the Simon Sinek tour: cancelled. And every single one of my other gigs, whether they be overseas or domestic, booked or merely pencilled in, MC-ing or keynote – all cancelled.

Social distancing was the new norm, and whatever else you might be allowed to do, the one thing you could write off for the foreseeable future was getting large groups of people together in one location to listen to a speech. I had more chance of earning a crust in Queen Camel. Hey ho, hey ho, it's off to work I didn't go.

And it wasn't just me. First Alex, then Harry, then Grace, lost their jobs. All within days of each other. Kate dodged the bullet by being put on one day a week, but with the best will in the world a one-day-a-week job wasn't going to provide for a family of six.

Only Eve retained some semblance of normality as she was halfway through her training to be a nurse, and if there was one thing the world looked like needing in this new reality, it was nurses. But as she was still training it wasn't a paying gig – so no relief there either.

Amongst all the chaos I tried to look upon my situation with a positive mindset and largely managed to avoid any existential and psychological trauma. Not just because others had it far worse, but because being isolated and without any official work structure or organisational framework is something I've learned to do, ever since the events I wrote about in *Fat, Forty and Fired.*

Back then when I was forty, I lost my job, had four kids under the age of six, was living in a foreign country with no support network, was fat with a drinking problem and – just when I thought things couldn't possibly get worse – was rushed to hospital for emergency surgery.

After serious reflection I realised if I was to save myself and loved ones from further disaster, there were two unavoidable steps to take. First of all, I had to *acknowledge* the full reality of my situation, and, secondly, *choose* a consistently positive mindset to attempt to improve that reality. Not to indulge in Pollyanna-ish bullshit, but commit to some clear-eyed, practical daily actions that would slowly and sustainably ameliorate my circumstances.

I had to take personal responsibility for the type of man I wanted to be, and the life I wanted to lead and legacy I wanted to leave. I think the US Navy Seals call it 'extreme ownership'. I call it: 'Getting your shit together and consciously choosing to make the best of the cards you've been dealt.' Every day.

So for the last few years my morning routine has begun with me quietly reciting the following poem to myself:

Every day is a fresh beginning;
Listen, my soul, to the glad refrain,
And, spite of old sorrow, and older sinning
And puzzles forecasted and possible pain,
Take heart with the day and begin again.

I'm well aware it might sound a tad pretentious. Guilty as charged. But as it doesn't harm anyone else and I find it genuinely helpful, I'm sticking with the routine. It's in the fabulous *Poetry Pharmacy*. I like the book so much I hunted down the author to appear on Five of My Life – still one of my all-time favourite episodes.

In some ways, that mid-life crisis year two decades ago not only saved my life at the time, it was also an invaluable dry run for this upcoming social isolation. It made me face up to being unexpectedly forced to stay at home with no job or work to go to – and, unlike then, at least this time I actually *had* a cabin to help me with the cabin fever.

34

The cabin

IT'S NOT REALLY a cabin. A cabin suggests attractive wooden walls, cutesy sloping roof, cosy fire, view of a lake and fresh coffee brewing on a stove.

My 'cabin' is the small storage room that the previous owners of our house had built underneath the carport. After opening the door, you can reach the back wall in three strides. It takes you less than one to travel the width of the space. As you're doing so, a tall person would have to duck their head – the flat ceiling being so low. The walls are bare brick, the floor worn lino.

There's no plumbing, stove or heating. Bizarrely, though, there are floor-to-ceiling sliding glass doors on one side. I say bizarrely, because if you were to open them and step out, as the design suggests you should, you would immediately fall ten or so feet to the ground below – there being no veranda, balcony or railing.

The view from the cabin isn't of a lake or forest; instead, the sliding doors provide a perfect frame for a close-up picture of the neighbour's rubbish bins – the sole vista aside from the outside wall of our downstairs toilet. It is also permanently damp, meaning our electricity bill is crippling large, because of the dehumidifier I have to have on year round to stop the place being overrun with mould.

And noisy? Oh boy, is it noisy. Built as it is into the hill by the main road, you don't just hear every car going past – you *feel* it. I swear my desk rattles when a truck thunders by. The room makes me think of that large dish antenna at the Parkes Observatory, which allowed the world to view the first moon landing. My cabin doesn't receive signals from space, but it does seem to magically pick up every couple's argument, child's cry, gardener's leaf-blower, bird's song, builder's radio, postman's whistle and barking dog within a 500-metre radius.

It is also home to a family of startlingly large geckos. They aren't dangerous, and I don't mind them, but they do tend to give you a shock when they suddenly appear out of one of the many holes that line the joining of the wall and floor.

But there is one detail about my study that is more important than any other. It has a door. Sweet Mary, Mother of Jesus – it has a door. PraisewhicheverGodyouworship, *it has a door*. A door you can open and close. And lock. Rarely, if ever, has a single object given me such joy as that plain, ugly rotting door.

One of my favourite stories in Winnie the Pooh is when the permanently gloomy donkey Eeyore has a birthday. He grudgingly allows himself a hint of excitement as he looks forward to his presents, but because of a series of mishaps all he gets given by his best friend, Piglet, is a pathetic, useless burst balloon. Rather than being offended or depressed, however, Eeyore spends the rest of his birthday putting it into – and then taking it out of – an empty honey jar (the poor bastard's only other birthday present), all the while contentedly noting 'Look, it goes in' and 'Look, it comes out again!'

It's how I feel about the door. 'Look, it opens,' and, more importantly, 'Look, it closes,' I giddily say to myself whenever I retreat behind it during agreed writing times. Without it, my hours there would be filled with endless stressful distractions. The door is utterly life transforming.

If the podcast roles were reversed and I was a guest on The Five of My Life, it would be my answer to the fifth 'possession' question. Because however noisy, cramped, animal-infested, ugly and damp my study might be, the door makes it *my* space. The space where I get to write.

I wrote large sections of my first book sitting on the floor of our then family kitchen – often with a coloured crayon on the back of one of my children's drawings, whilst pushing our baby twins' double rocking-chair with one foot and rolling a ball back and forth to our young sons with the other. Trust me, I've done the research. It's easier in a study.

To be able to construct, and protect, a workable regular writing routine is a privilege I'm undyingly grateful for. I realise most aren't lucky enough to have 'the door they can close'. Now that I am, I'm determined never to take my good fortune for granted and instead put it to good use.

I am extremely disciplined – when I decide to be. Kate thinks the second half is the most important, and maddening, bit of that sentence, but, whatever, let's just say I am extremely disciplined *when it comes to writing*. Not just with the daily routine, but with the ever-present accessories I require before I can put pen to paper or finger to keypad.

Every morning I'm at my desk by 9 am. Coffee in the same favourite chipped mug from Vietnam in my left hand, old leaking fountain pen of my father's in my right. Pebble picked up from a creek in Texas in my pocket. Desk clear, apart from an old laptop and a 15-centimetre-high stack of A5 paper in the middle of the left-hand edge.

This pile consists solely of paper that I have repurposed. I use a lot when I'm writing and a few years ago I decided that, rather than wastefully buy new paper to do this on, I'd keep every bit of paper I use – say, emails I've printed off or bank statements I've been sent – cut it in half, turn it over and use the other side. It's practical, it's a small action for the environment, and it's often fascinating reliving the memories the flip side of the paper I happen to be using that day generates. (Did we really always have so little money in our account, and I can't believe yet another person has written to me about my underwater photography being prominent among them.)

So it would be fair to say that my door, routine and accessories made me happy as a seagull with a French fry when writing alone in my damp study. Despite my personal happiness, publicly it somehow felt a little shameful that whilst others in the area were dressing in power suits and driving Porsches to their corner offices overlooking the harbour, I was walking eight steps in my dressing-gown to a semi underground hovel. So I kept my feelings secret and meekly accepted the occasional pitying looks I got from the masters of the universe, and their partners, as they busied themselves on their more conventional path.

That is, until it came up in conversation with my son Alex and I tentatively tried to explain to him how I felt about my study.

'Oh, I know exactly what you mean, Dad,' he immediately said before I'd even finished.

'Err . . . really, mate? How can you know *exactly* what I mean – I've only just told you.'

'Yeah, I know, but it's how Roald Dahl felt about his writing shed as well. I'll send you a clip.'

It's such a delicious moment when you watch or read something that sums up precisely how you feel about something you previously believed was your weird perversion – and yours alone. It is so normalising. So legitimising. Of your secret – and somehow of your entire self as well.

It's not just me – one of the greatest writers the world has ever seen also had a shitty 'cabin' he loved. And by the sound of things, it was indeed every bit as shitty as mine.

I learned from the video Alex sent me that for forty years Dahl wrote in a shed in his back garden in Great Missenden in the UK. By his own description it was far from palatial – the floor was covered in goat droppings, walls lined with ill-fitting polystyrene, spiderwebs in every corner, all the contents yellowing and smelling of cigarette smoke.

But, like mine, it had a door. A door which he could close and therefore forget the outside world and concentrate fully on writing, without fear of being disturbed. It was an intensely personal space, filled with objects that held special meaning for him; be it an opal sent to him by a child in Australia or a chip of his own hip bone after an operation. I suddenly felt less stupid about the piece of old driftwood a reader had sent me that I've kept on my bookshelf for the last twenty years.

Dahl spoke of his humble shed as 'my little nest, my womb'. No wonder Alex got so readily what I was trying to explain. And, rather affirmingly, as I investigated further I discovered Dahl also had his own idiosyncratic writing routine.

It included sharpening six pencils every morning before he started. Not four or five pencils. Six. And it made no difference if he didn't use any of them. Again, it made me feel less stupid about that pebble from Texas I had to have in my pocket and Dad's leaking fountain pen. Whenever I doubt how I've chosen to arrange my working life, my attitude now is that if it's good enough for the genius who gave us *James and the Giant Peach*, *Matilda* and *Tales of the Unexpected*, it's good enough for me.

It's a key lesson I try to communicate in my talks about work-life balance. There is no one answer to the challenge of *how* to work. You have to discover through trial and error what's right for you. And then have the courage to follow that, not slavishly copy what everyone else is doing, or feel bad that society seems to encourage a different, more conventional way of going about things.

It's up to each of us to decide on the type of life we desire and then entirely our responsibility to try to create that life and protect the boundaries it involves. No-one – not the government, nor your employer – is going to do it for you.

However, being happy about my working routine was one thing. Somehow earning enough money from that routine to provide for the family was another.

And not feeling guilty about being happy was another thing entirely . . .

35

Taking confession

WHETHER IT'S BECAUSE of my schooling, parents or just innate personality, I've always felt a bit uneasy about being happy. Like I was somehow letting the side down, not trying hard enough or, worse, being inappropriately and cold-heartedly unempathetic, given all the horrors and misery always happening to so many people somewhere around the world on any given day.

And this uneasiness was naturally heightened during 2020, when the general public misery of Covid combined with the specific personal upset of my mum's condition. My occasional feeling of genuine quiet contentment as I sat in my cabin writing made me somehow almost . . . morally uncomfortable. Like I was being a leaner not a lifter, by not joining in with the societal malaise. What possible right had I to be *enjoying* myself amid so much unhappiness?

It's a pretty important issue to address as you head into your third trimester. Not believing you have the right to happiness, or ever allowing yourself to feel contentment, is a pretty limiting attitude. And maybe an even more crucial question is how does it help others, and serve society generally, for you to be constantly miserable?

The respected psychiatry lecturer and author Paul Martin is one of the leading authorities on happiness. He has an interesting take on the type of uncomfortableness I was experiencing: 'Happiness is good for you, good for your children *and for society*, so don't be embarrassed about making it a top priority.' My italics.

I'm not talking about crassly rubbing your happiness in other people's faces. Or being smug or self-satisfied. I'm just recommending thinking about how best you can *actually* help. Focusing on those things you can control, not those you can't. And choosing not to put on false displays of anguish or moroseness as you do.

So I made a resolution – in the manner Martin suggests – to stop beating myself up when, in the midst of the two misery-inducing Cs of Covid and mum's cancer, happiness occasionally reared its smiling head.

36

A arhoswch heno?

THE COVID CHAOS made me think about the previous time
I experienced a global pandemic. It was the late 1980s and I
was living in London and working hard at my second proper
job. After a depressing, nugatory two years working on the
railways, I somehow landed an amazing role for the British
National Health Service.

I was the lowly advertising manager for a body called the
Health Education Authority – the job in which I briefly and
tragically reconnected with my childhood friend Tim. I say
'amazing role', as it was a rare combination of advertising
and doing good. Rather than selling shampoo – or, worse,
cigarettes – we were tasked with educating the nation on how
to be healthy. So I could have all the fun and excitement of
the advertising industry with none of the guilt.

More importantly, I loved learning the fundamentals of effective communication and persuasion. The strategic and creative skills necessary to produce powerful behaviour-changing advertising campaigns fascinated me. And because we were a government department dealing with vital, high-profile issues – such as smoking, heart disease, contraception – I was in an environment where we were lucky enough to work with massive budgets and some of the very best agencies in the world.

I was therefore in a rather unusual position when AIDS foisted itself onto the global agenda. Because of my role, I was present in meetings with the types of powerful people (government ministers, senior health officials and advertising agency CEOs) someone of my tender age and junior status would never normally expect to be. It was *the* issue of the moment. Nothing was higher priority.

No expense was spared and we had the brightest advertising minds of the day working for us. I was aware of how unique a time it was and determined to learn and contribute as much as humanly possible. It's an incredible feeling and privilege to work on something that actually matters to society as a whole and can save lives.

It makes what followed all the more devastating. After exhaustive research, we came to our key conclusion. The campaign everyone was talking about at the time was the one running in Australia. It used scare tactics (the ads actually featured the Grim Reaper himself) to communicate that *everyone* was at extreme deadly risk from this horrible new disease. Which was precisely the *opposite* of what we recommended.

We decided that a finely targeted set of activities was required in the UK, rather than a mass communication campaign to the population at large. At the time in Britain, the data was clear.

HIV and AIDS were solely present – and producing awful tragedies – in discrete identifiable communities. If we could quickly, clearly and lovingly take action amongst those groups, we would save the most lives and avoid wasting limited funds unnecessarily panicking the general population.

I thought it was hugely important work. However, when we made our presentation to the powers that be, it was a disaster.

'So you are recommending a series of targeted programmes?' the communications minister asked. 'Giving clean syringes to drug addicts, free condoms to prostitutes, education and support to the young male sexually-active homosexual community, and immediate auditing of all blood-transfusion services?'

'Yes, Minister.'

'And no mass-communication campaign.'

'Exactly.'

'That's madness.'

'I'm sorry?'

'Madness! I want to see proposals for a TV campaign aimed at everyone!'

It was awful to witness. It would be fair to say I lost my naivety that day; more accurately, it was belted out of me. The government was not interested in listening to what might actually work best. They had already made up their minds – and decided that politically they had to be seen to be doing something dramatic, extreme and for the entire population – not for particular sections of it.

Understandably, the gay community didn't want to be stigmatised by a government-authorised advertising campaign. But rather than take this concern fully on board and develop communication accordingly, the bizarre conclusion was not to target them. At times, it felt like I was in an episode of *Blackadder*.

'So, Baldrick, we know that the people most at risk are single, gay, sexually promiscuous males?'

'Yes, sir.'

'And your cunning plan is to ignore them completely and target heterosexual couples instead?'

'Yes, sir.'

Except it wasn't funny, because that's what we did. To cut a long and extremely painful story short, we followed none of our initial recommendations and, instead, ended up making a number of television commercials aimed at young heterosexual couples. The main message of which was that *everyone* was at risk. *Everyone* must use a condom. *Everyone* must practise 'safe sex'.

Eighteen-year-old virgin boy about to have sex for the first time with your eighteen-year-old virgin girlfriend? Yep, you. You're at real risk from AIDS and have to use a condom. Not a *Blackadder* sketch, but government policy. It was shameful, misleading and ineffective. And surprisingly long term as the politicians became trapped by their own hysteria. To moderate the message would be to admit their culpability in success-fully creating the damaging bandwagoning hysteria in the first place. So they kept banging the same old dishonest drum.

The final straw for me was the Kafka-like nightmare when we were asked to make versions of our television advertisements in Welsh. Although it's generally British Government policy to translate everything into Welsh, when we ran the media numbers we discovered that the proportion of the people we were advertising to whose primary language was Welsh was . . . 0 per cent. Nought. *No-one.*

We might as well have been doing the ads in Swahili or Inuktitut for all the good they were going to do. Clinging to a vestige of integrity and wanting to avoid expensive pointless work, we presented this information and suggested we could save the taxpayer some money, only to be told – you guessed it – to shut up and do it, anyway.

I've never forgotten the lessons I learned from the experience of working on that campaign. Amongst other things it has made me hyperaware of when someone, however unwittingly, starts to focus on *being seen* to be doing something, as opposed to diligently working on what might actually produce the desired outcome. More trivially, I also learned that '*A arhoswch heno?*' means 'Will you stay tonight?' So maybe the Welsh adaption wasn't a total waste of time, after all.

37

Esse quam videri

THROUGHOUT MY TWENTY-FIVE-ODD years in advertising, I was professionally involved in trying to help address a number of societal issues: drink driving, obesity, AIDS, vaccinations, heart disease, organ donation, animal welfare, smoking.

Outside of my communications career, I've also seriously engaged in three other issues: climate change, Indigenous education and body image. The first was through my role as one of the co-founders of Earth Hour, the second via my work with the wonderful Australian Indigenous Education Foundation, and the last as the creator of the Sydney Skinny.

In each of these cases the same lesson is learned afresh. Like the siren song calling ships to crash on the rocks, there is always the overwhelming pressure, when you are in the midst of one of these projects, to *be seen to be doing something*. And whatever the issue, the temptation is to talk it up, so it's taken seriously.

This leads to the people working on these projects making all manner of extravagant and alarmist claims. Forget balance, and sensitive targeting – the money, and attention, is in extremist language and absolutes. We are all going to die of AIDS, one in three of us have mental problems, the entire world is in danger of flooding in a decade, factory farming is akin to the holocaust.

'Raising awareness' is often the justification for such an approach, and at certain stages of an issue that is, indeed, appropriate. When, in its launch year, a journalist called Earth Hour 'merely an awareness-raising advertising stunt', I took it as a compliment. That was *precisely* my vision for it. Back then.

However, at some stage you have to move beyond awareness and seriously think about outcomes. The trouble is, though, that it's always easier to stay hiding behind simplistic alarmist 'awareness raising' as your objective, rather than developing strategies that stand a chance of helping to improve anything in the real world.

Perversely, you tend to get more credit for simply continuing to bang the drum about the generic problem than suggesting specific answers. Running an expensive campaign to raise awareness of the melting ice caps, or the fact that models on the front cover of magazines have all been photoshopped, is sure to get you a round of metaphorical societal applause.

However, at the same time it's painfully obvious, if you bother to look a bit closer, that it's achieving the square root of bugger all. We all know that the ice caps are melting and real women don't look like the cover girls. 'What are you *doing* about it?' seems a more valid question to ask.

The challenge is to resist the siren call and instead suggest a few solutions – solutions whose effectiveness can be measured, transparently and publicly. My dear friend and CEO of the Australian Indigenous Education Foundation, Andrew Penfold, has a mantra, 'Hard heads, soft hearts, capable hands,' which is as good as any I've come across to ensure that your efforts, however well intentioned, don't fall into the trap of being merely ineffective shouting. Or of throwing money at a problem with no evidence, or hope, of any actual progress.

Ever since my experience on that early AIDS campaign, I've always been suspicious the moment I see people making a dramatic noise about a generic issue. I try to force myself to keep an open mind and be intelligently questioning – not rush to pick up a Twitter pitchfork. What do the experts, not social media, say about this? Do any disagree? What's in it for the people who are making the noise? (Don't get me started on some of the condom or face-mask manufacturers in the AIDS and Covid crisis.) Are any solutions being proposed? How will their effectiveness be measured? Is there anything I can personally do to help improve matters? Or am I just being asked to panic and be depressed?

A little more balance and calm, measured thinking about doing what works – in other words, *esse quam videri* (to be, rather than to seem to be) – would achieve so much more.

Sometimes it's as if people like talking endlessly about a problem and wouldn't want it to be solved, because then they'd have nothing left to do or talk about.

Which somehow reminds me of the Australian Republican Movement.

38

The speaking
vacuum cleaner

WHEN I'M GIVING a speech or in a meeting, more often than not
I use a few personal stories to illustrate the leadership or business
points I'm trying to make. In this environment, the stories of
Nelson Mandela, Apple, Uber etc can often make an appearance, but I try to avoid them. My thinking is that it's a bit lame
to talk about things you weren't personally involved in.

One of my favourite tales describes an incident I was
involved in with the Hoover corporation back in the early
1990s. I was working for their advertising agency in London,
which involved frequent trips to their headquarters in the
Welsh town of Merthyr Tydfil.

On one such visit we were in the middle of presenting
some campaign ideas to the CEO and his team when we were

interrupted by an excited group of engineers bursting into the boardroom. Full of apologies for the disturbance, they breathlessly explained to the CEO that they simply *had* to show him the product breakthrough they had finally made. They invited me and my agency colleagues to gather round as well while they explained.

Remember this was over thirty years ago, when Hoover had an overwhelming share of the market: 90 per cent in the UK. And 100 per cent of those vacuum cleaners had detachable bags to collect the dirt the machines sucked up. When these bags got full, they either had to be replaced with new ones or emptied and refitted. The way in which you found out your bag was full was a small red light situated at the foot of the cleaner. Simple. And how things had been done for decades. Until now.

'So, you see this prototype has no light,' the head R&D manager said to the group.

'Indeed, Gareth, so how, pray tell us, will the housewife know when the bag is full?' asked the mildly irritated CEO.

'That's the thing!' he replied. 'By a voice saying, "Your bag is full."'

'How on earth will that work?' the CEO asked.

'Well, it took us a while but we've discovered a way to put a tiny recorder in the machine. Now, when the bag is approaching full, rather than the sensor triggering a small red light, it triggers a recording. Watch.'

He proceeded to plug the Hoover prototype – obviously pre-filled with dirt – into the wall and demonstrate.

I stood there, slack jawed in amazement, waiting nervously for the hapless R&D team to be sacked on the spot. Surely even a dribbling moron could immediately spot that this ridiculous invention was the answer to a problem that didn't exist.

There wasn't a vacuum-cleaner consumer alive who had any issue with a red light informing them their bag was approaching full. No car manufacturer in the course of history has ever thought to replace their petrol red light system with a spoken version. And besides, this was the era when other ambitious entrepreneurs were launching genuine disruptive improvements into the vacuum category, such as the three-in-one carpet shampoo/vacuum and James Dyson's bagless hoover. Meanwhile, these muppets were fucking around fitting tape recorders into their soon-to-be-obsolete products. Come to think of it, *I* wanted to fire them.

The reaction to the demonstration, though, was even more astonishing than the idiotic invention itself. Rather than the R&D team being given a flea in their ear and kicked out, the meeting descended into a joyous round of celebratory back slapping and high fiving – led by the CEO.

It should be no surprise that Hoover steadily squandered its market dominance and actually went out of business in the UK over the next few years. At least lives weren't at stake, as they were in my hideous AIDS meetings, but the level of incompetence was of a similar jaw-dropping level.

This brings me to the Australian Republican Movement. I am a proud Australian citizen and fully paid-up member of the republican movement. I applaud the energy, passion and dedication of those who work in the organisation. And I think it's absurd that we are in any way led by the British Royal Family. Which is why it pains me to say I feel the ARM may just have got the wrong approach.

As Churchill said, 'However beautiful the strategy, you should occasionally look at the results.'

As with my experience on that early AIDS campaign, the ARM have focused on talking up the problem. Time and time again, putting out messages about how awful it is that ultimately – on paper – we're ruled by the Royal Family.

But as with the ice caps and cover models, the issue is pretty self-evident. We already know that the current arrangement is outdated. And the confronting reality is, whilst I wish we weren't ultimately ruled by the Royal Family, we also know from our lived experience that on a day-to-day basis it is *not* awful that we are. Nothing bad happens.

No Australian's life is made worse by us being a constitutional monarchy, and it won't be made better when we become a republic. Monday will still be Monday and Tuesday will still be Tuesday. People will literally not be able to notice a difference. As with those Hoover executives, the ARM is in danger of solving a problem the audience don't have. The Australian public, rightly, has far bigger, more pressing, priorities. And again, I say this as someone who dearly wants us to be a republic.

The ARM seems to have made the mistake – all too common in business – of confusing outputs with outcomes. During the UK AIDS campaign, government ministers were quick to point out how many adverts had been made and leaflets distributed. Call me a bluff old traditionalist, but I think a better measure would be how many lives had been saved.

The ARM has one clear objective – make Australia a republic. You shouldn't judge ARM's success by how busy, noisy or productive they are. They have *one* job.

I fear also that the wrong tone is unwittingly employed. It is tempting but misguided to believe that to argue for a republic, you have to criticise Britain or the monarchy or the Queen. Why bother? It misses the point as much as a speaking vacuum cleaner. And runs the risk of making the ARM members look mean-spirited and dim.

I know a number of them and that couldn't be further from the truth, They are all charming, intelligent and generous. This is not about the people, it is about the *strategy*. If you are running up the wrong hill, being well motivated and hard-working doesn't help – it is still the wrong hill.

Creating messaging that is attention grabbing and high profile is easier (and more fun) than doing the complex, challenging, behind-the-scenes work of gaining clarity, alignment and commitment amongst *all* relevant stakeholders on the precise details of the system of government we would move to.

I'd recommend the ARM adopt a strategy that avoids any attempt to create a grass-roots movement. Or publicity or 'momentum'. As with climate change, I suggest the ARM would be better served by moving beyond raising awareness of the problem to a low-profile campaign that wastes no time on selling the concept of a republic. An action plan should simply assume a republic is obviously where we are headed eventually and in a calm way the ARM should work on the things that need to be done to make it happen soonest.

To those who might doubt the potential effectiveness of such an approach, I'd point out that, based on the single objective involved, it would be *impossible* to be less successful than the old campaigns. So why not give it a shot?

39

Queen Camel 5

WHILE OBSERVING THE lockdown rules might have been the responsible thing for me and Kate to do in Sydney, for Mum in Queen Camel it was genuinely a matter of life and death. She couldn't have been any more firmly in the bullseye of the highest risk category. Old *and* ill.

This nicely polished my guilt and discomfort about having flown home to Australia 14,000 kilometres away from her – leading me to redouble my efforts in trying to 'help'. Which, in turn, only made things worse.

When I was in Queen Camel, there was a variety of things I could do to try to marginally improve matters for her: be it shopping, making cups of tea, playing games of Scrabble, whatever. I was *there*, so I could do stuff. Now being so far apart, the only way I could see of making Mum's situation better was by intelligently and selectively putting the power of technology to work.

A few years earlier, Kate and I had bought her an iPad. It was the product of slightly delusional hope, given her previous treatment of the digital picture frame. And, sure enough, Mr Jobs would be turning in his grave as, in all the years of her ownership of said item, she had – how shall we put it? – 'significantly underutilised' the product's potential.

I'm not saying she used it as a chopping board, like those Italian grandparents in the YouTube video, but, given her actual behaviour, she might as well have. Despite the multiple functions of this piece of groundbreaking Apple hardware, my dear mum used it solely for email. No internet, no podcasts, no films, no FaceTime, no photos, no games, no maps. Just email. And not in the way that you or I might use email.

Mum's unique approach to this electronic wonder was to never generate an email, but only reply to them. And never – *never* – 'reply all', always responding only to the singular sender. In all the years of sending Mum emails cc'ed to my brother, he'd never received her replies to me. The same applied to the ones he'd sent her.

After our repeated attempts to talk her through how to generate an email herself and showing her how to press 'reply all', and repeated failure for it to result in any change to her emailing skill set, we dropped it. As with the picture frame, it was her life and it wasn't mission critical.

But now, with her health combined with the extreme isolation measures she had to follow, it seemed to be the perfect, indeed essential, time for us to step up and enable her to get more benefit from the technology at her fingertips.

Weeks earlier, my brother had got Mum's house properly hooked up to wi-fi, so the only thing now standing between her and the world of entertainment and connection offered by the miracle of the internet was attitudinal, not technological. Given Mum's attitude, however, no small ask.

Taking it very gently, we started with the top three things we knew Mum liked and valued, and which we thought would make the most difference to her life: Scrabble, grandkids and Radio 4.

Mum used to host regular Scrabble afternoons with a group of friends in the village, so we talked her through how – by placing her finger on the yellow 'Words with friends' square that my brother showed her on the iPad screen – she could still play with the group every Wednesday, but without leaving the house. She could even play with her younger son in Sydney.

She missed seeing her Australian grandkids, so we demonstrated to her how FaceTime worked. During this dry run, we emphasised that it was entirely *free*.

Lastly, we explained how, by pressing the BBC podcast button, she could access all the fabulous programmes she loved to listen to on Radio 4 at any time she liked. Never again would she miss an episode of *The Archers* – the legendary BBC drama that has been broadcast since 1951 – or have to stay awake to catch a play on the radio. It was all there at her fingertips whenever she wanted it, courtesy of her iPad and wi-fi connection.

I have to admit I felt pretty pleased with myself. I had no doubt those three things alone would transform her day-to-day life whilst she struggled with the twin demons of isolation and illness.

However, the truth is that sending the *Hindenburg* to rescue passengers from the *Titanic* would have been more of a success than our 'Improve Mum's happiness by getting her engaged with the gifts of the online world' meddling. She resolutely ignored all three of our suggestions.

It would have been easier to take if, for some reason, she'd overtly *refused* to engage with them. Instead, though, she agreed they were all good ideas when we were explaining them to her – and then simply did nothing about them.

This is the most devastatingly effective way of getting out of a request to do something. Because if you disagree with me, I'll debate you and try to convince you of the wisdom of doing whatever it is I'm asking. Whereas if you nod along, saying, 'That's nice,' I'll assume the message has been success-fully received and will be acted on. Rookie error.

It's sad because I do feel her life could have been made tangibly and significantly brighter, more meaningful and less depressing if we'd been more successful with our well-intentioned, but ultimately hapless, intervention.

My failure really upset me and I couldn't help spending a lot of time thinking about it.

40

Granny Vi

WERE WE JUST doomed to repeat the same mistakes generation after generation down the ages? The Marsh family has a painful history of being idiotic when it comes to embracing technological advances. One of the anecdotes that looms large in Marsh family folklore is the one about Granny Vi and the video recorder.

Granny Vi was my mum's mum, a lovely soul who never said a bad word about anyone her entire life. A real salt of the earth type, she lived all her life in the country house she was born in. She never owned a fridge, had central heating or drove a car. She had strong values, a loving heart and simple tastes. And one of those tastes was *Coronation Street*.

Coronation Street is the world's longest-running TV soap opera. Long before Australia had *Neighbours* and America had

Days of Our Lives, Britain had *Coronation Street*. Debuting in 1960 there have been well over 10,000 episodes.

For twenty-five-odd years, Granny Vi rarely missed one of them. And the reality throughout those twenty-five years was that if she did miss an episode, she'd really missed it, as this was long before Netflix, IQ or even the internet. And it was one of the few things that properly bothered her on these infrequent occasions.

So you can imagine how certain my parents were that they'd nailed it in the birthday-gift stakes when, one year in the mid-1970s, they decided to buy her a VHS video recorder. The price of such a device had recently plummeted, but it was still an unusually expensive gift for us as a family. However, Mum and Dad were simply so excited to be able to deliver Granny Vi a 'guaranteed-never-miss-another-episode' future that they couldn't help themselves.

They bought a stack of blank video cassettes and my brother and I wrote 'Coronation Street' on all the labels. And on the day itself, we distracted Granny Vi so Dad could fully install it, with all the correct wires, remote control and batteries, to make sure it was simple to use from the moment we revealed it sitting beneath her TV set.

And how was it received? She *hated* it.

'But, Ma, it means you'll never miss an episode,' my bewildered mother pleaded after the gift's icy-cold reception.

'Umm . . .' Granny Vi replied.

'And it won't cost you anything.'

'Umm . . .'

'You needn't stay in if something else clashes with your favourite programme.'

'Umm . . .'

'It's super-easy to use. All you have to do is press this button.'

'Umm . . .'

'And you won't have to buy any cassettes. Jomma and Nidgey have got you all you need here.'

'Umm . . .'

'Ma, *please*. At least let me show you how to use it.'

'Not now, dear, it's lunchtime,' Granny Vi replied, closing down further discussion of the offending item.

And she never used it. Not once. Ever.

It almost sent my parents potty. It was a good four hours drive to Granny Vi's house and one of my strongest childhood memories is of the drive home that day.

I was ten, my brother twelve. We sat in the back seat of the old family car, barely able to see our parents through the clouds of smoke from Dad's chain smoking.

We could certainly hear them, though, as the whole way home they spoke animatedly about how closed-minded and stubborn Granny Vi was. How she was cutting herself off from so much enjoyment. How only she would suffer.

The stream of angry, hurt, disappointed venting was interrupted every fifteen minutes or so by Mum turning around and saying to Jonathon and me, 'Now, boys, I want you to promise to never let Daddy or me get like Granny Vi. Promise me.'

'Yes, Mum,' we'd reply in unison.

'And if we do, you'll tell us, won't you?'

'Yes, Mum. Promise.'

On it went the whole journey. We must have promised twenty times not to let her 'get like Granny Vi and the video recorder'. And yet here I was, decades later, looking at a moth-balled digital picture frame and an underused iPad.

Talking to Kate, she told me an almost identical story about her grandad and dad – except their offending technological breakthrough was a hearing aid. Both simply refused to use one well past the point of stone deafness.

For a while, I thought that maybe the issue was simply the inevitable result of new technology being too challenging for elderly people, and I should just get over myself. Until I spoke to my friend David about it.

'It's not technology,' he said. 'It's more complex than that. I've got similar challenges with my dad. He's getting on and finding it increasingly difficult to cope.'

'And you're trying to get him on the internet?'

'Oh no, nothing like that. He loves the internet. What's difficult is trying to get him to consider changing his daily routine slightly. He's eighty-nine and not able to do all the things he used to do. He gets tired, overwhelmed and stressed, trying to fit it all in.'

'Not being rude, mate,' I said, 'but what exactly are all these things he has to do?'

'Precisely my thoughts. I visited to try and understand better. It turns out that every morning for the last twenty-odd years, since he downsized to the unit, he's been cleaning the floors – all of them – daily. And not just sweeping them. He *mops* them as well.'

'Blimey, we're lucky if we mop ours once a year.'

'Yeah, it is ridiculously excessive. And, at his age, obviously the reason he finds the rest of the day so exhausting.'

'So what did you do?'

'Well, I didn't want him to think I was ordering him around or forcibly taking charge, so I suggested he think about cutting back to mopping the floors every other day, instead of every day.'

'Sounds sensible. How did that go down?'

'Well, it's the weirdest thing. He just looked at me. And didn't say a word. In fact, he didn't mention it at all – until the next morning, when he looked at me with what I can only describe as mild contempt and said the problem wasn't *him* cleaning the floors every day, it was *my* low standards.'

'Ouch.'

'And that's not all. He went on to tell me that when he and Mum visited us in Rockery Court once, our place was filthy.'

'Rockery Court?' I said. 'You haven't lived there for over thirty years!'

'I know. Bizarre thing to bring up after all these years. Especially as I'm pretty certain we always kept our house clean and tidy then, like we do now.'

It made me feel lucky that my mum only 'consents and evades', as opposed to the 'attack and insult' approach.

So, between the VCRs, online Scrabble and squeaky-clean floors, I think there must be valuable lessons to be learned to help us avoid the same mistakes and enjoy our old age more. Why do so many old people find it impossible to change?

I know it's easier to point something out to someone else than to implement it yourself. Also, that in many cases there are complex issues at play, regarding a fear of losing control or insensitive children unpleasantly bossing parents around. Or a lack of empathy leading to a misunderstanding of what's really going on. Maybe David's dad mopping is his secret and sacred way of honouring his beloved late wife?

But, with love in my heart, I sincerely believe that – in my mum's case, at least – a large reason for her intransigence was closed-minded, stupid stubbornness: pure and simple. It crept up on her increasingly during her sixties and seventies, until it was habitual and immovable in her eighties. And I was partly to blame because I clearly failed with the promise I made in the family car all those years ago.

That failure meant that her stubbornness negatively impacted her quality of life just as it did Granny Vi's. And just as it will have a negative impact on Kate's and mine, if we allow ourselves to slide into the same bad habits over our later years.

But how can you stop yourself slipping? It clearly happens even when you're determined for it not to. At the time, Mum wasn't joking with her plea to us on the journey back from Granny Vi's. Yet, decades later, here she was, refusing to listen, engage or try anything new – despite the repeated best efforts of those who loved her the most.

Try as I might, and with a worrying sense that history might merely repeat itself, I simply haven't been able to come up with a better strategy than also begging our kids, 'Promise not to let us get like Granny.'

Credit to them – the early signs are that they're equal to the task of breaking the generational cycle of Marsh technological pigheadedness. They have an advantage, because, for as long as I can remember, they've accused me of having a cymbal-banging monkey in my brain, like Homer Simpson, that starts up whenever I get even slightly bored or confused with a topic. So they're well practised at recognising the signs.

'Dad! The monkey!' they yell, whenever they sense me start to tune out. Given that I'm convinced of the benefit – now and for the future – of forcing myself to stay open-minded, I try to follow their direction, even though it frequently makes me feel uncomfortable. And occasionally stupid. *Very* stupid.

I recently mentioned to them that the lovely people who do my podcast for me had requested that I change my email signature to include the link to the 5ML Spotify playlist. A totally reasonable suggestion. And one that I'd been studiously ignoring.

Embarrassingly, a) I didn't know how to do it, and b) I feared it would take me hours to work it out if I tried.

'Dad, they're right – you *should* do it,' Alex said.

'Umm,' I replied.

'Seriously.'

'Not now, mate. Not enough head space today. Maybe next week.'

'This is ridiculous. You tell us to tell you when you're behaving like Granny and FaceTime – well, you are now.'

Reminding myself of my promise, I resolved to step up. 'Okay, mate, I promise I'll do it today.'

I cancelled the meeting I had that morning, made myself a strong cup of coffee and mentally prepared myself for three or four hours of humiliating torture as I was put through the IT wringer.

Sitting down at my desk with an open mind and a determination not to give in – no matter how complex or numerous the technological hurdles – I turned on my computer and opened my email.

Right there in the top right-hand corner was a little drop-down box that said 'edit signature'. *Funny, never actually noticed that before.* I clicked on it and copied and pasted the Spotify link. I then sent an email to myself to test whether it had worked, convinced that I'd somehow fucked it up and would have to spend the rest of the day at the Apple store to rectify the situation.

But no. *Ping*. There was my email and at the bottom of it my new correct signature. I hadn't even taken a sip of my coffee. The whole process couldn't have taken much more than one single minute.

What. A. Moron.

If, as a near-sixty-year-old, that was my thought process about doing something that turned out to be so simple, how dare I be so harsh to my dear mum when I failed to get her to use her iPad properly.

I've resolved to learn the lesson and focus on my attitude to change and 'new things'. It's in everyone's interests if you sort out your unhelpful attitudes and bad habits *now*. Before your third trimister – not to wait for your eighties. By then, you're probably too set in your ways and it's likely too late to change.

We need to recognise the bad habits we're exhibiting and developing at the *start* of the third trimester, so we can take action to stop them significantly affecting our enjoyment of life at the end of the trimester – and in the process avoid driving our own children insane with frustration.

If I was reluctant to listen to advice on how to change my email signature when I wasn't yet sixty, what the hell am I going to be like when I'm eighty? I don't think it is sensible for me – or fair to Eve, Grace, Harry and Alex – to find out.

41

Frog

ONE HABIT I definitely need to change now, before it gets too late, is my eating. Or, more accurately, my snacking. Snacking on confectionery.

The extent of my problem was brought into sharp relief the evening I returned home from my routine nightly dog walk, car keys in hand, to be met by a quizzical Kate holding our dog, Mattie, and saying, 'Did you forget something?'

Now before you condemn me for walking the dog without either a dog or a walk, context is important. Just like the young friend of my nephew who knocked on my brother's front door to be met by my brother hissing, 'And you can fuck off as well, you chavvy twat!' you need to know what had been happening *before* he opened the door – or before I mistook going for a drive alone as 'taking the dog for a walk'.

For the past seventeen years, until the sad passing of our beloved Mattie, I had two daily rituals that were set in stone. One, in the morning, was bringing Kate a cup of tea in bed. The other, in the evening, was taking Mattie for a walk. The first ritual has stayed the same for thirty years. At the time agreed upon and double checked the night before, I place a cup of tea on the table on Kate's side of the bed and she murmurs, 'Not now, too early,' turns over and goes back to sleep. Ten minutes later, she moans, 'Tea – I need tea,' upon which signal I make her a fresh second hot cup and remove the cold one. Every. Day.

The other ritual has, shall we say, *evolved*. It started with me walking the dog with one or more of the kids. Such a lovely way to end the day, spend relaxed time with them, chat and mess around. Then one evening, while throwing a tennis ball for Mattie, Alex said, 'Dad, shall we walk home via The Friendly Store tonight?'

The Friendly Store is our local mixed-business corner shop that happens to have an excellent selection of ice cream and chocolate.

'Sure, mate, good idea,' I replied.

That became the new routine – walk the dog with son or daughter in the sure knowledge that we'd return home munching on an ice cream or chocolate bought from The Friendly Store.

Then, a bit like the cliched story of the frog in the pan of slowly heating water, the incremental changes kept coming. Rather than walk the dog to the beach, then go to The Friendly Store, we cut out the middle man and walked directly to the shop and back. It was still a walk for Mattie, but not really the original idea.

One day we jumped giggling into the car with the dog and drove, rather than walked, to the store – it was raining, after all, Mattie was getting old, and we needed to hurry before the shop closed. Besides, who was keeping score? And so on until eventually, this particular evening, I'd inadvertently dispensed with the walk, child and dog, as my routine had embarrassingly morphed into me simply driving to the shop for chocolate before it closed.

I never said I was perfect.

42

Buddha

My night-time 'dog-walking' trips, and penchant for sugary treats generally, meant that, not to put too fine a point on it, I was fat. Not as fat as when I wrote *Fat, Forty and Fired* all those years ago, but all the same I was decidedly soft around the edges and a not so proud owner of a pronounced beer belly. The latter wasn't just unsightly, but ironic, given my ongoing twenty-year abstention from the amber nectar.

My eyes were opened to the potential root cause of my seeming inability to keep to a sensible weight and shape when I read David Gillespie's *Sweet Poison*. The book spoke so clearly to my behaviour. I'm not sure I'd go so far as to label my imbibing of the white stuff – in confectionery and otherwise – as an addiction, but my relationship with it sure as hell wasn't healthy. After all, I'd never driven to the corner shop, in a panic that it might already be closed, to buy broccoli – broccoli that I'd then stuff into my mouth before I'd even got back to the car.

I suspected I needed to address this behaviour and its results *now* before it was too late. Apparently, it becomes so much harder to drop the pounds as you age. Losing 15 kilos at sixty is hard but doable. At eighty, it's nigh on impossible – and why bother anyway? It was starting to feel like this was my last realistic chance to stop the rot.

There's a picture of me from forty-odd years ago, on some beach in the Middle East, that Kate occasionally taunted me with. I'd been doing manual work out in the baking weather for months. My hair was long, halfway down my back, and bleached strikingly white by the desert sun. Along with the manual labour I was on a pauper's diet, so I was slim. And, much to Kate's amusement, I had what could be described – if you squinted a little – as a sixpack. It wasn't your full Hemsworth, but a flat stomach whose muscle definition couldn't simply be explained away by the fact that the picture had been taken by a girl I was trying to impress and therefore I was secretly sucking in my stomach and tensing my muscles so hard I was about to faint.

Every now and then, Kate would wave the photo at me and not so subtly ask, 'Where's *my* sixpack, you fat bastard?' The question – strangely usually asked when she saw me waddling with intent towards the bed – combined with a remark from my brother whilst on a recent walking holiday ('Nigel, you have the body of a god. Not a Greek god. Buddha') stiffened my resolve to take action and reverse the decline.

I harboured no illusions of regaining any former nineteen-year-old ripped glory. Instead, I set myself a goal of being my ideal weight by the time I published this book – in little more than a year's time. Not as a short-term, unsustainable milestone, though. I wanted to permanently reset my norm, addressing my sugar habit at the same time as regaining a trim, healthy figure to take with me throughout my old age.

I was careful in defining my ideal weight. One of the previous stumbling blocks had been deciding on unrealistic targets that merely set me up for failure. '*Well, it was a silly target, anyway*' was my ready-made excuse for quitting.

I spent a bit of time researching what was an appropriate goal. Just as I didn't want to set a delusional 'Ryan Gosling's body by Christmas' target, I also didn't want to limit my aspirations and accept the other non-Hollywood American standard that being *merely* 15 kilograms overweight was fine. Just because society had let its standards slip didn't mean I wanted to.

Being trim and having a flat stomach wasn't too much to ask. Well, not if you were Kate doing the asking, it wasn't. I resolved to lose 15 kilos by publication date. And as a firm believer in the business mantra that 'What gets measured gets done', I decided – in direct contradiction to all the official health advice – to use solely will power and the scales to get me there.

On my fifty-eighth birthday, I started weighing myself every morning and keeping a note of the number. As someone wiser than me once said, 'You become successful the moment you start to move towards a worthwhile goal.'

43

Top 50

THE FORTY-YEAR-OLD SLIM picture got me to thinking about former glories, not just in regards to my weight but *in regards to everything*. The photo was only one of an increasingly large and frequent series of reminders that my best days were behind me. Every week I found myself bumping awkwardly into evidence of my growing obsolescence and irrelevance.

There was a brief period in my early fifties when, through a happy series of accidents, I had enjoyed a modicum of success in a couple of fields. My book was amongst the Top 10 bestsellers, I was CEO of a firm that was doing well, and a TED speech I had given was gaining global attention. All of this culminated in my inclusion on a list that my kids had recently found on the internet and regularly – and with great hilarity – enjoyed reminding me of at our dinner table.

'Hey, Dad, who would you say were amongst the most influential old people in the world *today?*' Eve would ask, winking at her sister whilst waving a printed-off copy of the offending list.

'Yes, Nigel, who do you think,' Kate would add (rather unnecessarily, I thought), 'would be *forty-ninth?*'

An online community called High50 produces a list every year of the top fifty most influential people in the world over fifty. Or at least their opinion of who they are. And back in 2012, alongside the likes of Angela Merkel and Meryl Streep, was yours truly. It was a bizarre list, to say the least, but irrespective of what drug the judges must have been smoking when they included me, if they were to repeat the process today, I, and my kids, were well aware I wouldn't make the top 50,000, let alone fifty.

Ever since *Fat, Forty and Fired*, I have followed an unconventional career path. My attitude was perfectly described by the Russian poet Yevgeny Yevtushenko, when he said, 'I shall therefore pursue my career by not trying to pursue one.' Despite my laissez-faire approach to such matters, I still enjoyed being called up by corporate headhunters from time to time, sounding me out about my interest in whatever role they were spruiking. It made me feel not so much important as remembered and respected.

Over the years, however, the time between those calls has got steadily longer and longer, until now I haven't had one for over a year. In the sexual sphere I'm told they call that a 'reclassified virgin', making me a 'reclassified don't-call-us-and-we-won't-call-you', I suppose.

Weight, career, exercise – in all areas of my life it seemed I was playing a shameful game of loss and decline. And that the playing fields were now being occupied by more youthful and relevant participants. Every day, I saw younger people doing far better in their jobs than I ever had.

I remember the very morning after my fifty-eighth birthday, I read in the business press that one of the graduate trainees who used to work for me in London was now the firm's global CEO, with an office on the top floor of a skyscraper in New York. And here was I in my dressing-gown, sitting in a damp cabin under our garage in Sydney. Graham Greene might have got the wrong decades when he said that life is lived in the first twenty years and the remainder is just reflection, but I knew what he meant.

And yet . . . there also seems to be a monumentally important life lesson here. It is a huge mistake to equate your most successful days being behind you as your *happiest* days being behind you. For a start, our memory is a notoriously unreliable instrument – full of inaccuracies, distortions and wishful thinking. In truth I wasn't *that* successful, or permanently blissfully happy, in earlier years. And clinging to an idealised version of the past makes it more likely you'll be dissatisfied with your present – and the prospect of your future. Whilst I'm pretty certain my most conventionally successful days *are* behind me, I'm also equally optimistic my happiest ones are in front.

Conventional success is just that. There's nothing wrong with it; indeed, lots great about it. But it's finite, there is no finish line, it isn't a guarantee of happiness and it doesn't last. You can't live life at peak intensity. Nor at peak success.

My friend Todd, who has climbed Everest amongst many other notable achievements, once said to me, 'No-one can live at the top of the mountain forever.' We can't all get to the summit, and those who do can't stay there. To chase a never-ending series of career – or other – highs is the road to deep misery.

You have to come to terms with the natural ebb and flow of your life. Sure, enjoy the temporary good times and lucky breaks if and when you're lucky enough to have any. But don't expect it to make you happy – many people are surprised when they're made deeply miserable by their conventional success. But even if you have some success *and* it makes you happy, don't expect it to last or try to replicate that success repeatedly throughout your third trimester. You'll merely be setting yourself up for failure and a world of pain.

The sadly departed American neurosurgeon Paul Kalanithi said, 'The future, instead of the ladder towards the goals of life, flattens out into a perpetual present.' And that is no bad thing. The task is to work on enjoying that present, not constantly pining for a mythical future full of milestones that will magically make you content and fulfilled. A psychiatrist friend tells me there is a clinical term for this syndrome – arrival fallacy – and that a growing number of her clients suffer from it.

All these musings were crystallised at the most unlikely of occasions, when Kate and I went to a Don McLean concert . . .

44

American Pie

Don McLean was playing at the Enmore Theatre in Sydney. It's one of my favourite venues – having bags of character and offering great views to the stage – but with the best will in the world not the size and quality of venue McLean would have been used to in the USA at the peak of his fame. That peak, however, was half a century ago.

Talented artist though he is, McLean never managed to replicate his early success, and despite releasing over twenty albums he is still, unfairly, regarded by some as a bit of a one-hit wonder: that hit being, of course, the fabulous eight-minute-long Buddy Holly tribute, 'American Pie'.

So, like Sisyphus rolling the boulder up that hill in Greek mythology, he has spent decades playing to audiences, most of whom have only really come to see him play 'American Pie'. It's a song he's played tens of thousands of times before, and at the Enmore in 2021 exactly fifty years after he released it, I was fascinated to see how he dealt with this never-ending crushing public reminder of his former glories and of his best days being behind him.

On a rainy evening, he came on stage to rapturous applause. Taking the mic from the stand, he thanked us for making the effort to come out in the dismal weather, telling us that it was such a privilege to be able to perform to audiences like us around the world.

Then he added, 'Don't worry, I'm not going to make you wait until the encore for "American Pie". I'm going to play it twice – once halfway through my set, and then also in the encore. Hell, if you yell loud enough, I'll even play it again!'

He then launched straight into his other hit single, the Vincent van Gogh tribute, 'Vincent'. And for the next two-and-a-half hours, he had the audience in the palm of his hands. I've been to a lot of live music and this truly was a sensational performance, up there with the very best. The energy he brought and the connection he created was a wonder to behold. He actually looked like he was loving life and genuinely enjoying every minute.

A cynical friend who I told this story to informed me that McLean travels the world with his new girlfriend and that's the real reason behind his sunny disposition. That partner is a Playboy model forty-eight years younger than him, who wasn't even born when 'American Pie' was released.

However, I chose a deeper, more uplifting narrative. And I don't care if I'm right or not – a positive one serves me better as a motivating example to learn from and strive towards.

I choose to believe that McLean has long since come to terms with the reality of his situation, and he's grateful for his past success and for the life it has afforded him. Going forward, he has resolved not to moan or worry about his absence from the music charts. Instead, he has noticed the simple fact that no recording artist in human history stays at the top forever. There is always a newer, fresher act that claims the crown. Only to then be toppled by the next person soon after.

McLean has taken a look at his lot, focused on the positives and decided to make the best of his situation, working out how to create a fulfilling 'perpetual present'. Rather than setting the goal of matching or topping past achievements, he concentrates on the challenge of continually engaging and connecting with audiences, however small and far flung they now might be, and giving each and every one of them a great night. With that perspective, a trip to Sydney to play a concert could be viewed with relish, not dread – irrespective of any accommodating Playboy bunny in tow.

Forget the truth of McLean's motivations. I believe this issue is one of *the* keys to having an enjoyable and meaningful third trimester. In your first and second trimester, your life is inevitably punctuated with momentous, externally observable and therefore rewarded, milestones. It is natural, sensible even, to be focused on the next tangible step 'upward'.

From getting out of nappies, to learning to ride a bike, to leaving school, to your first proper job, to getting married, to being promoted at work so you can afford a down payment on a unit, etc – whenever you reach one goal or target, it's immediately replaced by another from a list that is seemingly endless.

But it isn't endless – it just feels like that on your way to thirty, and then through to sixty. But once you get to sixty, for the vast majority of us all that has changed. It's highly likely that you'll never again get a bigger job or larger salary or better body or gain dramatic public praise.

You. Have. Peaked. And that's fine. Or should be with the right attitude.

There is a real value and nobility in getting up in the morning and cheerfully doing the best you can with what you've got – without excelling or seeking attention – before going to bed and starting all over again the next morning. And I'm not necessarily referring to paid employment. It could be being a good dad or supportive partner or helpful neighbour.

There is a wonderful Buddhist phrase, 'Before enlightenment – chop wood, carry water. After enlightment? Chop wood, carry water.' No matter our position on the ladder of conventional success, we've all still got to sit down to go to the loo, face ourselves in the mirror, lay our heads down to sleep at night, and wake up each morning one day nearer our death.

At some stage we need to come to terms with life and become the people we were meant to be. Or, in many cases, the person we have been all along but might have lost sight of. To be able to go about your business with a smile on your dial, comfortable in your own skin, causing no one else harm or drama, and maybe even making a few people slightly, briefly, happier is a heroic achievement.

The philosophy of enoughness is hugely undervalued. I've come to understand that to construct a life where you don't 'live for the weekend', but regularly find joy in your Tuesdays and Wednesdays, is one of life's great accomplishments.

45

Cate Blanchett

KATE MAKES A fair point when she suggests that maybe my new-found, hard-won 'wisdom' about old age is partly a cloak I wrap around myself to protect me from the increasing cycle of disappointments, frustrations and defeats that would otherwise drive me insane.

If part of ageing successfully involves making peace with failure, few things could be better training than trying to make a movie. No, that's not strictly true – if you are Steven Spielberg or Tom Cruise, making a movie must be a cross between a walk in the park and a laugh riot. If you are Nigel Marsh, on the other hand, it's a pride-swallowing siege (to quote Mr Cruise's character in *Jerry Maguire*). A siege that lasts not years, but decades. I realise this is an absurdly first-world problem. I'm not after sympathy – I don't deserve any – instead, my interest is in the potential learnings to take into my third trimester.

The failure isn't the worst part. It's the hope. In the first flush of *Fat, Forty and Fired*'s success, film makers came a'knockin'. I simple-heartedly and naively believed that when they said, 'We'll make a movie of your book,' they meant, 'We'll make a movie of the book.' Rookie error.

What they meant was: 'We'd like to *try* to make a movie of your book.' As a result, for years I was the classic example of Churchill's quote, 'Success consists of going from failure to failure without loss of enthusiasm.'

I remember how excited I was when Warner Bros signed up the movie rights in 2006. And as the time passed between the rights being sold and the movie not being made, in the face of all available evidence I kept the faith. Every time Kate asked me how the film was going, I'd confess my ignorance and call up the producer. And every time I did, I'd come off the phone bubbling with excitement at the latest titbit I'd been fed.

'It's going great, sweetheart,' I'd say.

'Really?' Kate would reply. 'It seems to me like the square root of bugger all is happening.'

'Yeah, I know it *looks* like that, but Paul Rudd is interested in playing me and about to sign on.'

Paul Rudd never did sign on. So a few months later, Kate's questioning would make me call again.

'You'll never guess what?!' I'd breathlessly relay. 'Hugh Grant is reading the script as we speak!'

'Yeah, right, and Elvis is alive and living on Mars.'

'No, really. He insisted everything is going great and it's going to happen. Defo. Guaranteed.'

'You're so gullible, Nigel. Every time you call, they just string you along by name dropping someone famous, and you go all goo-goo-eyed and weak at the knees. Get real, it's been years. They clearly can't get the funding and they're no nearer making it than they were back then.'

And, of course, she was right. Hugh Grant didn't sign up either, so yet again I'd call up to inquire about any progress. Eventually, the penny started to drop, and one day, after my latest conversation with Warner Bros, I was slightly less enthusiastic as I reported back to Kate.

'I think you're right, sweetheart,' I admitted. 'Nothing of substance has happened and it doesn't seem like it will.'

Kate nodded sympathetically, but knowingly.

'They did mention that Cate Blanchett was interested in playing your part, though.'

'Really?' Kate's eyes lit up. 'Cate Blanchett playing me?'

'Yeah. Apparently they want to "make the narrative arc crisper" – whatever that means. So the plan is to get an old, fat, ugly actor to exaggerate my decrepitude and Cate Blanchett to emphasise your youth and beauty.'

'You know what your problem is, Nigel – you get too cynical and easily discouraged. It all sounds rather encouraging to me.'

Surprisingly, though, Cate Blanchett didn't sign up either. And here I am, twenty years after publishing *Fat, Forty and Fired*, having sold and extended the film rights three times to three different companies. And still – apart from literally hundreds of conversations in which I've been told everything is 'going great' – fuck all has happened.

Over the years, I've talked to numerous people more experienced than me about this humiliating extended failure and it's been fascinating. The first told me that – for ordinary mortals; not the Cruises of this world – making a film is like trying to cook a steak by placing it on a table in the next room and, every now and then, asking different people to open the door, go in and briefly breathe on it.

One friend who works in the business helped me see the process from the other side. I asked him why people in the industry would string me along with all the BS about things 'going great'.

'The thing is, they aren't stringing you along,' he explained. 'When they're being enthusiastic about the latest supposedly exciting development, they genuinely believe it.'

'So why do none of the things they say happen?'

'Well, there are obviously hundreds of different possible reasons, but one thing you've got to watch out for is their rose-coloured language. When they say, "Cate Blanchett is going to play Kate," what that probably means is that they *have* sent the script to Cate Blanchett. But it also means they have bugger-all idea if she has even seen it, let alone read it or liked it.'

Another friend recounted the story of the making of one of my all-time favourite films, *One Flew over the Cuckoo's Nest*. Given that it was based on a sensationally successful book, had Jack Nicholson in the lead role and that Michael Douglas owned the rights, I'd assumed its transformation from page to screen would have been a swift one.

Not a bit of it. It turns out that the original purchaser of the rights was *Kirk* Douglas, who sold them on to his son when he couldn't get it made after years of trying. All told, the process took twelve years.

If those A-Listers took over a decade to get it done, just maybe there is actually hope for me. After all, I've recently been told that everything is going great and Russell Crowe is reading the script.

46

Whitewater

As I'vε sαid, the reason I tell the story about the utter failure of my film career isn't some tin-eared plea for sympathy. Or because I actually find it quite cathartic to do so. (Although I do.) No, the reason I tell it is because I'm keen for this book not to indulge in any Pollyanna-ish 'Old age is all wonderful' narrative. It isn't. Lots of old age sucks. And blows. At the same time. And in so many ways.

For starters, my hearing is going, so I constantly have to ask my friends and family to repeat themselves; or worse, to avoid being irritating I pretend I can hear and miss out on genuinely meaningful interactions. Also, it's a good night when I haven't had to get up more than twice to go to the loo; my knees mean I can no longer play squash, a game

I adored; if my gums recede any further I'll start looking like one of Damien Hirst's skull sculptures; barely a month seems to go by when there isn't at least one doctor rummaging around up my backside doing a colonoscopy, looking for a polyp, examining a prostate or some such. I could go on.

In fact, now I mention it I *will* go on. My earnings are falling and have been for years; it's becoming increasingly obvious we haven't got enough pension and it's too late to meaningfully address that; we'll soon have to sell the beloved family home; my short-term memory is fading; headhunters never call; I'll be dead before my film gets made; my short-term memory is fading; young women in the street or park overtly adjust their underwear in front of me, because, to them, I am literally unimaginable as a flesh-and-blood male; I increasingly fret about getting dementia like my dear late dad; my face has so many wrinkles that pictures of me from my London days don't look like a younger version of me, they look like a completely different human being; it's too late to fulfil a number of dreams, like getting to see David Bowie in concert; everything is sagging, however many weights I lift; the pace of technology is baffling; new music sounds awful; younger people have started to say 'Okay boomer' to me (me too – I had to look it up); I'm going to more funerals than weddings; I'm losing my hair . . .

The cherry on top was during my last visit to the dentist. She tried to sound reassuring when she said, 'Ah, wait a minute. We'll have to quickly take a picture of that.'

'Picture of what?'

'The brown dot on the roof of your mouth, so I can send it to the specialist to check.'

'Check what?'

'Oh, that it's not what it's unlikely to be.'

'And what would that be?'

'Well, I don't want to worry you.'

'Too late. So, go on, what are you checking isn't in my mouth?'

'Well . . . err . . . mouth cancer.'

Marvellous.

So it's undeniable that old age is full of its fair share of challenges and downsides. But here's the thing. It is equally undeniable that *so is every other life stage*. Life is constant whitewater – there simply isn't any age in which you haven't got problems, challenges, worries and disappointments.

We tend to forget this and romanticise our younger years when we look back from old age. But, looking back honestly, our teenage years were full of angst: why do girls not fancy me? Will I ever fit in? How long will this acne last? Do these exams never end? Could my parents be any more annoying? How can I ever afford to buy a car? And so on.

The issues don't stop when you move into young adulthood. Will I ever find lasting love? Can I even get pregnant? Is there a career for me that doesn't involve soul suicide? Why is my boss such a dickhead?

But the wonderful flipside of the rather sobering inventory above is that every life stage also has fabulous bits – including old age. Especially old age. Because just as being young has its unique upsides, so does old age. If you do it right, and have a bit of luck, you're more comfortable in your own skin; you care less what other people think of you; you've worked out who your real friends are; you're more mindful about how you spend the precious time left to you; you're less easily embarrassed; you're smarter, kinder, gentler; you haven't got to spend your life commuting to a crushingly pointless job, or working for an arsehat; you take deep pleasure in trying to help people who you feel deserve it; you're more accepting of others; you're more accepting of yourself; you have a calm perspective that only sixty years of lived experience can give you; you're more grateful; you're less sexually repressed; you're less defensive and a better listener; you've let go of any debilitating notion of perfection; you've nothing to prove to anyone; you're more in touch with your creativity; you have the freedom to devote proper time to getting *really* good at a hobby; you're more moderate and open to compromise; you find yourself laughing more; you're more honest with yourself and others; the memories of three decades of creating and nurturing a family provide you with wonderful memories that are accessible whenever you choose; you have grandkids, sons and daughters in law to look forward to; and to cap it all off, you experience the deep, liberating and lasting joy of allowing yourself to be the person you really are.

So I suppose the lesson here, or one of them, is we should stop romanticising youth and catastrophising old age. Life just *is*. And if we concentrate on learning how to calmly accept the inevitable bad bits, and focus instead on the equally inevitable good bits, we'll all be a damn sight happier in our third trimester.

Irrespective of whatever the dentist might happen to discover in your mouth.

47

Tamed by a Highlander

EVERY MONTH OR SO I catch up with a bunch of dads from my sons' old school to share a curry and have a natter. They're a relaxed and varied bunch. We're all of a similar age and life stage. And lifestyle. Or so I thought, until Matt — a divorced member of the group with a new girlfriend — under innocent questioning unwittingly revealed just a little too much for comfort.

'You look sore, mate. Done your back?'

'Yep. Nothing too bad. Just got to take it easy for a week or so.'

'Put it out at the weekend?'

'Yep. Wrenched it.'

'Golf?'

'Err . . .'

'Surfing?'

'Err . . .'

'Gardening?'

'Err . . . just a weekend away . . . you know . . . with Rosemary . . .'

'Ah,' the table fell awkwardly, but respectfully, quiet as five dads' shoulders slumped slightly. Thoughtful expressions crossed our faces as we mentally compared Matt's imagined activities on his loved-up dirty weekend with our own slightly more mundane exertions.

Of course, one of the many casualties of increasing age is romance. Or it can so often be. Especially if you're in a decades-long monogamous relationship.

Kate and I have been husband and wife for over thirty years and, given we got married when I was twenty-eight, it means I've been a husband for longer than I was single. It would be fair to say that, every now and then, something reminds me I might need to raise my game in the romance stakes.

In 2021, to celebrate our wedding anniversary I booked a lovely rustic restaurant in the Blue Mountains. I made sure we had a secluded cosy table by the log fire and the owners knew it was a special occasion, so they could add a few touches to enhance the mood.

Over the main course I could see Kate worrying away at one of her back teeth with her tongue, and uttered the immortal words, 'Sweetheart, I've got some inter-dental probes in my briefcase in the car, if you'd like me to get you one?'

Nice? I like to think so. Romantic? Not so much.

But truth be told, at the age of almost sixty, and after thirty-odd years of partnership, romance and sex aren't always the very first things on either of your minds. I was reminded of this reality last summer when standing by the Bronte beach pool with two friends, watching the local rugby league team do their post-game rehab.

Basically, the rehab involved fifteen or so incredibly fit and buff men standing waist deep in the pool, so the cold water could work on repairing their sore legs. This, of course, meant there were fifteen sixpacks and thirty muscled, often heavily tattooed, arms on display.

When I busted my twenty-year-old friend sneaking a few pictures on her phone, I exclaimed, 'Beki, are you doing what I think you are?!'

'Just a few – they look so hot.'

To which my other, fifty-year-old, female friend remarked, 'Those were the days. Now I just look at them and hope they've had a good breakfast, put enough sunscreen on and remembered their lunch money.'

It might be the case that, in your twenties, your days would be regularly punctuated by spontaneous sex in some of the most uncomfortable places – on the stairs, in the car, at the office or on that hike through the national park. In your sixties, there tends to be more of a build-up needed, comfortable surroundings preferred, and an occasional aid to get one in the mood.

Our kids take delight in retelling the story about a ten-year-old Harry picking up a paperback from Kate's bedside table with a painting of a fierce, dashingly handsome, Braveheart type on the cover and getting the pronunciation wrong – by mistakenly rhyming 'tam' with 'ham', when he innocently asked, 'Mummy, what's "*Tam*med by a Highlander" about?' I'm still not totally sure, but I'm guessing he doesn't need any inter-dental probes when he's tamming the object of his affections.

Underneath the humour there's a serious point here. Like any other area of life (fitness, finances, friendships, etc), long-term romantic relationships require constant effort and thoughtful prioritisation if they are to go the distance. Yet so often the signals we are sent is that your love life is the one area where 'it' just happens – with no planning, discipline or compromise. Your partner is 'hot' and love is in the air, and if your tummy doesn't get butterflies every time you see him or her, it's over and you are no longer 'in love'.

Such bollocks. But it's such a prominent societal cue, and so horribly damaging. I remember my father-in-law's speech at his fiftieth wedding anniversary, not just for the excellent opening joke ('I'm on the prune and Viagra diet – I don't know whether I'm coming or going'), but for the serious bit when he said, 'People say marriage is not a sprint, it's a marathon. They're wrong. It's a steeplechase.'

The whole 'falling in love' phrase is problematic. Usually, it actually means falling in lust. There's nothing wrong with that, but it's important not to confuse the two. Lust is a feeling. Love is a *decision*. And in a long-term relationship the focus should be on growing in love. Proper love, not 'magazine love' – or 'potato love' as Saul Bellow memorably called it.

The divorce rate in Australia, and worldwide generally, is truly saddening. Not because I'm against divorce in principle but because, in my mates' experience the divorce process is more often a barbaric slaughterhouse for everyone involved than it is a blissful Gwyneth Paltrow conscious uncoupling.

The writer Deborah Levy put it wonderfully when she wrote, after her own separation, 'I will never stop grieving for my long-held wish for enduring love that does not reduce its major players to something less than they are.'

I'm not the bloke to give the advice needed. I wouldn't dare. Kate and I will probably be divorced before this book is published, anyway, given 'Cushiongate'. This being the habit she has of insisting on buying utterly ridiculous large cushions – not pillows, cushions – that we have to put on our bed *on top of the pillows*. It drives me to question the very point of my existence.

I'm reliably informed that, in a healthy relationship, it should always be the couple versus the problem, not the couple versus each other – but in this case Kate doesn't see the problem, which takes the problem to a whole other level.

Irrespective of our own relationship's future success or failure, my *intention* is for it to get better as we get older, not the reverse. As Robert Browning said, and as I quote to Kate in my more soppy moments:

> Grow old along with me,
> The best is yet to be

48

Murder

'I WILL LEGIT do all the washing up and take the bins out for the rest of the year if someone kills Martin.'

It wasn't the usual type of message I received on our family 'Marshmellows Messenger' group chat, but the start to my day nevertheless. Our younger son had been out on the tiles the night before, and was now nursing a ferocious hangover. One of our neighbours – who clearly kept different hours – was indulging his passion for his leaf blower. At 7 am. On a Saturday. Using what must have been the loudest machine ever manufactured. And for *so* long.

It was as if, after he finished clearing his back garden, he was then blowing the leaves off the surrounding trees just so he'd have more to clear up. Murder was probably a bit extreme, but to be fair to Harry, it was something we'd become increasingly aware of in recent months.

'Oh Christ, he's started again,' one of us would say, prompting us all to walk around the house closing every window.

'Why don't you say something to him?' a friend asked, when she was visiting during one of his blowing sessions.

'We've thought of doing that,' I replied, 'but it never quite seemed the right time.'

'And we've never really got over the dog incident,' Kate added.

'What's the dog incident?'

Ah yes, the dog incident.

'When we moved in years ago,' Kate explained, 'a yuppie couple four doors down had a beautiful pair of large retriever dogs. They would both drive off to work early in the morning and then, from the moment the car left to the moment it returned, their dogs would bark incessantly. All day. Non-stop.

'It was so bad, not just for everyone within a hundred yards who had to listen to it, but it felt cruel for the dogs themselves. They sounded so distressed. The thing is that the couple themselves never heard it, because it only started after they'd driven off and stopped the moment the dogs heard the car return.'

'So what did you do?'

'Well we agonised about it for weeks, and then one evening I cracked and sent Nigel over with a bottle of wine.'

'And how did that go?'

'To be honest, I thought it went great,' I told our friend. 'I didn't pile in all guns blazing. I was very mild and friendly about it, approaching it from a concern for the dogs, not as a complaining neighbour. I made a couple of gentle suggestions about maybe hiring a dog walker, because having two large dogs locked up in a small backyard all day might not be helping matters. They seemed in happy agreement, they drank the whole bottle of wine, and we parted on the best terms.'

'And that sorted it?'

'Well, yes,' I said, 'but not in the way I'd imagined. Three weeks later, a "For Sale" sign appeared outside their house and they never spoke to me again. They moved out before the end of the year.'

To be honest, embarrassment over the dog incident wasn't the full explanation as to why we hadn't confronted the leaf-blower issue.

There was another more important reason. My father always used to say to me that, after your health, one of the most essential elements of a happy life was having good neighbours. And he was very particular with what he meant by 'good'. He didn't mean people who became your best friends, who you had dinner with twice a week and went away with for holidays.

Instead, he meant having people either side of you who were friendly, respectful, kind and helpful. People who smiled and said hello in the morning, who'd put your bins out and feed your cat if you were away, who'd keep a spare set of house keys for you, bring round a muffin or two when they had some left over – basically, people who were *neighbourly* in the proper sense of the word.

He maintained if you had that you had won the lottery of life. And we indeed have been blessed. Our neighbours have been wonderful for all the years we've lived here. And I would go to extreme lengths to keep it that way.

I would do almost anything to maintain things on a friendly neighbourly level – because the alternative is so utterly appalling. We know a number of people who've fallen out with their neighbours over something utterly trivial who then have their *entire existence* blighted by the fact that they don't speak to the people next door. Or, worse, in some cases are at war with them.

We have one set of friends who lived in the type of palatial house Kate and I could never imagine ever affording. It was a beachfront mansion in a ritzy suburb. They'd worked all their lives to be able to buy this, their dream house. Were they happy? Were they fuck.

They'd got into a protracted legal dispute with their next-door neighbours. And here's the thing. The dispute was about where each of them placed their bins at the end of their shared driveway for rubbish collection.

'You're joking!' I exclaimed, when they told me.

'Unfortunately I'm not. It started so small and then just escalated.'

This couple seemed to have everything – happy marriage, health, financial security, rewarding careers, dream house – yet the wife was driving to work in tears and the husband spent every weekend glaring miserably over the garden fence at his legal opponent. Madness. In the end, they put the house on the market and moved out four months later.

It's all too common a scenario. And, as I say, one I'd do anything to avoid – including deciding to uncomplainingly listen to a chuffing leaf blower. Every. Single. Weekend.

49

Family Rescue

LEAVING ASIDE MISATTRIBUTION of my underwater photographer skills, one of the joys of the internet is that people, if they so wish, can get hold of you. From anywhere in the world. In my childhood, of course, it would have been unthinkable that, with barely a few minutes effort from the kitchen table, I could strike up a conversation with someone I admired in another country.

Now, however, if you like – or indeed dislike – someone you've seen or read about, you can simply google them, and nine times out of ten, you'll be able to find an email address for you to send a message. I've done it myself on a number of occasions with wonderful results – striking up a number of lasting relationships with people I would otherwise never have met.

It's nice as well, on those rare occasions when it happens the other way round. I've long had a policy of replying to every email I receive. It just seems the polite thing to do. To my mind there is no downside to chatting with someone new who reaches out to you – at least once.

It doesn't take long, is never boring, often hilarious, and almost always I learn something valuable. It can also be fabulously surprising. My approach is to be open-minded, expect nothing, assume positive intent on behalf of the stranger and just listen.

So when I received an email recently from someone named Dan in New York, who claimed to have enjoyed my TED Talk, asking if we could set up a Zoom call to chat, I replied that it would be a pleasure.

'Thanks so much for agreeing to chat, Nigel.'

'No worries, Dan. You wanted to chat about the TED speech?'

'Ah no, not really.'

'Oh, okay – how can I help?'

'Well, have you heard of *Queer Eye for the Straight Guy* and *Supernanny*?'

'The TV shows?'

'Yep. That's what I do. I make reality TV in the US. Those are two of mine and I'm in the process of creating another series called *Family Rescue*. Having read your books, that's what I want to talk to you about.'

'Go on.'

'The show's premise is that we introduce the audience to four or five families who are doing it really tough and struggling. Not enough money, too many kids, father usually hasn't got a secure job, stressful present, uncertain future. You get the vibe.'

'Sure do.'

'In the early episodes we'll watch as four experts get to know these families and offer them advice on how best to deal with their situations. Then over the following twelve or so episodes, we'll join them on their journey to see how they go improving their circumstances.'

Trying hard not to be offended that he thought the Marsh family, as described in my books, were obvious candidates for such help, I tried a tactful deflection.

'You say this series is for the US market – but why would a US audience be interested in an Australian family?'

'Sorry?'

'Well, to be honest, Dan, I'm not convinced your viewers will care much about a family living in circumstances so different to theirs. Sydney is a long way away, and very different, from LA or New York. It's really nice of you to think of us, but all things considered, I reckon you'd be better off sticking to US families.'

Dan sounded shocked. 'Oh no, Nigel, you misunderstand me. We don't want you to be one of the families. We'd like you to be one of the experts.'

Fuck. Me. Dead. I wasn't expecting that.

Quite frankly, it was all a bit surreal. My TED Talk and books had made him think I could *give* advice, not receive it. Leaving aside the questionable assumption that I have the remotest credibility as an 'expert' in anything, to my mind there was an even bigger problem.

'Dan, forgive me for asking a silly question, but doesn't the fact that I'm white, middle class, middle aged, married and heterosexual make me ever so slightly not on trend within the current zeitgeist?'

'Oh no, Nigel, on the contrary – *you* would be the diversity on the panel. All the other judges are very on trend.'

It felt kind of weird and mildly belittling to be a quota filler. But a useful learning experience nevertheless.

All in all, it was a fascinating, surprising and hilarious conversation. At the end, I actually agreed to do a casting session with his colleagues in Los Angeles the following week. Owing to Covid, it would be via Zoom.

As it turned out, the technology wasn't a problem. The first question, however, was.

'So, Nigel, tell us why you want to be on a US reality TV show.'

On reflection, perhaps I was a little too honest.

'I don't,' I replied. 'It's not something I've ever thought about doing and, with respect, the genre isn't really my cup of tea. But when I explained this to Dan last week, he said it would still be appreciated if I at least agreed to have this chat.'

It went downhill from there.

When Kate asked me how it had gone, I broke it to her as gently as possible that her idiotic husband had fucked up the interview and our financial woes weren't going to be solved any time soon by me landing a lucrative American TV career.

It made it all the more surprising when, three weeks later, an email came through saying that I'd made the cut and asking where they should send the non-compete contract. It was a slightly unnecessary bureaucratic hurdle, because Kate Moss having my love child was more likely than me being asked in the following nine months to host 'any other major US television productions'.

Irrespective, sign it I did. I'll let you know how I go. The most likely scenario is that the series gets funding for its first season on the sole and strict condition that the Australian expert is replaced with someone more suitable, quick smart.

And who knows, if the worst comes to the worst, maybe the Marshes would benefit from some expert help, US reality style. Especially if the cushions-on-the-bed situation continues to escalate.

50

La La Land

Despite the unlikelihood of the American reality show ever amounting to anything, it did make me reflect on the notion of rolling the dice generally. Especially for someone approaching their third trimester without a conventional career.

I've always been strangely comfortable with the notion of 'absorbing uncertainty', believing that no-one can see into the future, and agonising about a decision doesn't necessarily make it a better one. I'd rather make a swift decision and get on with my life – living with the consequences, good or bad.

Kate claims this is all just a lame excuse for the fact that I'm lazy and often can't be fucked to consider decisions properly. But while, in part, she might have a point (the 'Stupid' part in this book's title), overall I feel she's wrong. Especially because as I look back on the last half century, I realise almost all of my best decisions (including asking her to marry me) have been when I've trusted my instincts, bet everything on red, backed myself and gone for it with gusto.

As the poem says

> Reason is a servant
> Intuition is a gift
> We've made the servant the master
> And forgotten the gift

However, it's one thing to respond to opportunities appropriately; it's quite another to operate in a way that maximises the chances of those opportunities actually presenting themselves to you in the first place.

I'm not talking about some of the more fanciful beliefs about the Law of Attraction that some dubious YouTubers like to spruik. I'm talking about the evidence of my own experiences, and while there are no guarantees and it involves a little effort, I'm convinced a subtle change in attitude and behaviour can tangibly affect the number and frequency of options you get to choose from.

Basically, I think if you adopt a permanent and default 'open-for-business' mindset, following through on that mindset will increasingly put you in the path of future opportunities. I'm not talking about being pushy or desperate – or worse, inappropriately bringing business matters into relationships that should remain strictly non-commercial. I'm talking about proactively putting yourself out there. Constantly rolling the dice – with no expectations, but with keen attention and a positive attitude towards whatever life might place in front of you.

The chances of meeting someone romantically are limited if you never leave the house and do anything new. And the same is true in a professional business sense. Wonderfully, the reverse is also true.

Of course, when you go to different places, mix with varied people and try new experiences, the chances of you meeting a romantic partner are drastically increased. Ditto for business opportunities – however surprising those opportunities might be. It's not the reason I reply to every email I get, but the many friendships and experiences created over the years by doing so are a welcome, and much appreciated, by-product.

A guest on the 5ML podcast was the futurist and author Dr Keith Suter. For his film, Keith picked *La La Land*, and the reason behind his choice was both surprising and powerfully affirming. He didn't choose it because of its swag of Oscars, but because of an early scene featuring the song 'Someone in the Crowd'.

Dr Suter explained that, to his mind, this scene 'sums it all up'. So much so that he uses a sixty-second clip from this scene when lecturing his students at Boston University about how best to find employment over the duration of their careers.

He is someone worth listening to on this topic, as for over half a century he has never had a conventional career, yet he's always been in work. And the majority of the multiple jobs he's had have come from opportunities that presented themselves seemingly from 'left field'. Suter would disagree, explaining that he has always made sure to adopt an attitude and behaviour that maximised the chances of those opportunities crossing his path.

The scene Suter was referring to is the one where Emma Stone can't be bothered to go out. She doesn't want to attend the party she's been invited to, preferring instead to stay in and flop on the sofa in front of the TV. Her flatmates dance around to 'Someone in the Crowd', trying to persuade her otherwise.

They explain that if she comes with them to the party she might (I'm paraphrasing) meet someone who could lift her off the ground, and maybe take her where she wanted to go.

It is, indeed, an excellent summary of the philosophy I'm talking about. I like to think of it as having 'humble strength'. You've got to turn up. Put yourself out there. Not with cynical intent or with the unrealistic expectation that you'll always get what you want, or what you expect, but turn up nevertheless, comfortable with the uncertainty and an openhearted 'open-for-business' mindset. If you do, you can relax about any particular outcome, and focus instead on being fully present in the moment for its own sake, and letting what will be, be.

51

The Five of My Life 2

I MIGHT HAVE been surprised by the Podcast of the Year award after ten episodes, but as we approached the fiftieth episode of the show, I was even more blindsided by the conversation I had with the media partners who'd produced and distributed it for me from the very beginning.

Usually, I dealt with the producer of my show, but the big cheese who ran the division that looked after all their podcasts had booked this meeting. He's a lovely bloke and I'd always enjoyed our interactions in the past, especially given my previous career in the media, so I was looking forward to the chat.

Things were going well across all measures – audience feedback, monthly downloads, advertising revenue – and I felt

I'd been improving as an interviewer. In the early podcasts, I'd developed the bad habit of swapping stories with my guests – as if we had equal billing. Over time, though, I began simply to commit wholeheartedly to the conversation in a curious, fully present manner – actively listening and extending the chat with follow-up enquiries, rather than relying solely on a set list of questions.

On one such occasion, much to my producer's horror, when a guest mentioned he used to have a job with John Lennon and Paul McCartney, I was so focused on getting through my list of questions that I replied, 'Interesting. Now, moving on to your fourth choice on Five of My Life, could you please tell us about the place you've chosen.'

Not good. But hey, an opportunity for personal growth, as the Americans say.

I was quietly proud of the work I had put in. Maybe the meeting was to congratulate me on my development? Or the six-month sponsor we had secured? Or the biggest audience two months in a row that we'd just enjoyed?

Nope. It was to cancel the show.

Pride comes before a fall and all that. I was devastated. Crushed.

He was extremely nice about it, but the simple fact was that Five of My Life wasn't big enough, quick enough, for their business model. The silver lining was they were extremely generous in giving me the rights to all the back episodes.

My desire to keep doing the show until I fall off the perch was as strong as it had always been, so my task was to find a new home. The process of finding one was fascinating. I was determined not to waste a crisis and instead use the slap in the face as a learning opportunity.

I made it my mission to talk to as many people in the industry as possible, and in doing so a clear theme was revealed. All the conversations were around how to make the show get *more* downloads to attract *more* advertisers to secure *more* revenue. And there was agreement on how to do this – *more* episodes, *more* frequently.

Which is precisely what I didn't want to do.

I didn't want The Five of My Life to be a weekly podcast. Nor did I want my focus to shift from having the best, most interesting conversations possible to worrying about the numbers. My attitude was slow and steady, concentrate on the quality and integrity of the show, and the followers would come. I realised this was hardly a drawcard for the big media players.

But it was important to me – and not just because of my desire to protect my original vision for 5ML as a show people looked forward to, rather than were bombarded by. As I approach my third trimester, I've developed an aversion to the 'more' word. I understand in many circumstances, it's a great objective – more empathy, more listening, more kindness – and that ambition, competition and drive can be wonderful. But as a blanket approach to everything, 'more' is a disaster.

I mentioned earlier a fabulous book called *Slow*, written by one of my guests on 5ML, Carl Honoré, which details the dangers of having 'fast' as your guiding principle. I believe slavishly following 'more' as your lodestar is equally dangerous. All too often, it creates a destructive, self-liquidating, soulless treadmill.

You could move the Olympics to every two years, not four. Then maybe every year. Wouldn't that be great? Of course, despite any short-term financial gain, it would simply end up destroying the specialness for fans and therefore value for advertisers. It happens all the time.

Don't get me started on Super Rugby, a loved tournament for many years – involving teams from Australia, New Zealand and South Africa – which has experienced plummeting interest recently, due to a 'more' strategy. More games and more teams has simply resulted in fewer fans and sponsors.

Crucially, 'more' is often a disaster in so many different personal areas. More alcohol, as I can attest, tends not to end well. More money doesn't fill a personal void of purposelessness. More romantic partners won't make you feel more loved. More spare bedrooms won't necessarily make you happier.

And on a broader societal level, 'more' on its own is often simply missing the nub of whatever issue we're struggling with. More roads don't guarantee less traffic. More channels don't guarantee better TV. More food produced doesn't guarantee fewer starving people. More houses don't guarantee less homelessness. More money doesn't guarantee better educational outcomes. And on a broader level still, globally more consumer consumption is helping us destroy the planet.

Whichever level you look at it from, I believe, especially for our third trimesters, we need to stop worshipping 'more' and work on an appropriate philosophy of enoughness. As long as the quality is there, scarcity adds – not subtracts – enjoyment and specialness. Treasuring, protecting and nurturing what you've got, instead of trying to constantly grow or monetise it, can lead to far greater contentment, meaning and value for all concerned.

By the way, I'm not saying I want to do *fewer* 5ML episodes. As far as the podcast is concerned, I'm not talking

'Less is more', I'm talking 'Same is best'. I think how I've designed the show is just fine and I believe it should be left as it is.

I tried this line of argument out on Kate.

'I hear you, Nigel, but it sounds a bit like you're bone idle and scrambling to justify the fact that you've been fired. Again.'

Ouch.

52

Brooklyn

As a family we decided a few years ago to attempt to limit the rampant orgy of overindulgence that, alarmingly, had crept into the Marsh family Christmas present-giving tradition. With the best of intentions, we had unwittingly been swept up in a sort of gifts arms race.

It got to the stage where every year Kate and I would spend a fortune sending expensive gifts, in wasteful packaging, across the oceans to far-flung nieces and nephews who hardly knew us and, truth be told, probably wouldn't appreciate the panic-bought offerings from their distant uncle and aunt, anyway. It was no-one's fault but our own, so we decided to take action.

Interestingly, when we did, there was a palpable sense of relief. It seems like we weren't the only ones with the 'This is getting ridiculous' feeling.

So, we've ended up with a state of affairs where we don't buy presents for anyone overseas and, instead, do Secret Santa within the immediate family. This involves drawing lots to find out which two members of the family you're secretly responsible for supplying with a Christmas present each.

Buying for only two members of the household, not five, was initially a bit weird – especially when I didn't draw Kate's name out of the hat in the first year we tried it. But it soon just became our new Christmas tradition and felt natural.

The savings to the family budget are significant and I like to think that the benefits to the environment, although small, are meaningful as well. However, the biggest upside of our new tradition isn't financial or environmental – it's the mindset it engenders. Rather than being a stressful, expensive and wasteful chore often done in auto-pilot, it's turned into an enjoyable, thoughtful process. One that we can really engage with in an authentic loving way. With only two gifts to get, we find ourselves giving proper thought to what the people whose names we've drawn might *really* appreciate.

And, boy, did Kate nail it last year. I was intrigued by the newspaper-wrapped gift she handed me on the day. It was so small and light, it couldn't have even been a paperback novel. To be honest, a rather shameful and hypocritical thought briefly flashed through my mind that maybe this was taking our new pared-back present philosophy a bit far.

How wrong could I have been? Because, when stripped away, the newspaper revealed a five-by-seven-inch blank booklet and accompanying leaflet, explaining that I'd been entered into the Brooklyn Sketchbook Project.

I'd never heard of it, but it turns out the idea is that you give someone a sketch journal and they fill it with their drawings – of any quality and any subject. They then send the completed book to New York where – and here is the incredible bit – your book gets stored in the Brooklyn Art Library. Forever. For anyone to view, from anywhere in the world, for the rest of time.

It is the largest collection of artists' sketchbooks in the world. At the click of a mouse you can view all of the more than 25,000 – and growing – held in the library. Having rejected Kate's title suggestion for this book, it seemed fitting to use it on this occasion – so if you search 'Celebrating, Sixty and Saggy', you can even view mine.

The project is run as a nonprofit organisation with the mission of 'allowing anyone to be creative'. I think it's a sensational idea and find it, and initiatives like it, enormously uplifting. There is simply no downside to projects like 'Poems on the Underground', which soothes commuters on their way to work in numerous cities around the world every day, or 'Sculptures by the Sea', which provides a platform for millions of people to enjoy works of art each year for free. They have such a lasting, positive and inclusive effect.

I have the greatest admiration for the founders and organisers behind them, people who often dedicate years of their lives to thankless, unpaid work that provides uplifting enjoyment for thousands of people and quietly makes the world ever-so-slightly better for generations to come. In many ways, they're the inspiration behind wanting to make my own small contribution with endeavours such as Earth Hour and the Sydney Skinny. But the Brooklyn Sketchbook Project has a special place in my heart because of that 'allowing anyone to be creative' mission.

The creative world can be so elitist and exclusive and off-putting. It's understandable to an extent – we can't all expect to be Michelangelo, nor should we be encouraged to delude ourselves that we are. But there's a huge difference between recognising that you aren't unusually *talented* and believing you aren't creative.

Everyone is creative, whether they know it or not. You're born creative. You literally have no choice. It pains and saddens me when I hear people say, 'Oh, I'm not creative,' when what they probably more accurately mean is, 'I've been led to believe my efforts are stupid, so I've lost any confidence in my ability and therefore my right to even try, hence I'm no good at it.'

Humans can be unwittingly crap sometimes. People should be enthusiastically encouraged to express themselves creatively, but the trouble is that, in our *America's Got Talent* world, people confuse that with 'and then impose my creativity on other people'.

I'm talking about being creative regularly, despite the knowledge that you're probably rubbish. And doing it anyway. And not feeling the need to show anyone. Or get anyone's approval. It is the private doing – the process of creative expression – that is the important thing. I don't believe we're fully alive if we haven't got some form of regular creative outlet. And drawing is such an accessible creative form that is available to everyone. With two entirely different benefits.

The first is the general substantial benefit you get from the 'beginner's mindset' whenever you attempt humbly to embrace any new skill – be it juggling, surfing, knitting, whatever. With the right attitude, the learning process itself is enjoyable. Being good at something isn't the only point of doing it.

If you have the attitude of merely privately and authentically engaging with a regular creative craft, there are few simpler, purer pleasures than putting marks on a page that, for you, have meaning of some kind. Representing what you see with an image made by your own hand is immediately and deeply satisfying.

The uncomplicated act of making some lines with a pencil and being able to recognise that, yes, it is that chair or dog or tree can improve any day, however foul your mood. And, dare I say, it is in many ways its own form of meditation.

The second benefit is difficult to explain – and believe – unless you actually do it. Learning to draw enhances your life. Yes, I understand the eye rolling, because I was once cynical about drawing, but I think that when you draw regularly a whole new world opens up for you. It improves your thinking. You become more adept at problem solving. You start to calmly accept challenges and mindfully ponder the best way to deal with them. You become increasingly observant, noticing things you've never seen before and – perhaps more importantly – viewing things you've seen a thousand times before in new fresh ways.

You also tend to develop more patience. Things, or people, that you might previously have written off as boring become intriguing puzzles to look at, and listen to, ever closer; trying to find the interesting, rewarding angle that is inevitably there – if you give them enough patient, curious, quality attention.

And finally, for many it sparks the realisation that every moment you're granted on this earth is a moment of creation, and that each of these moments contains infinite possibilities. You start to view your own life as a work of art for which you, and you alone, have the responsibility, and privilege, to draw to the best of your ability.

Evidently, re-reading that last paragraph, unfortunately it can also lead to one being rather pretentious – so apologies for that. Nevertheless, I hope some of you are encouraged to give drawing a go, despite my flowery proselytising.

53

The Sixth Regret

ONE OF MY guests on The Five of My Life was the delightful Bronnie Ware. Bronnie attracted global attention when, after a number of years tending to the dying as a palliative nurse, she published a list of the common regrets her patients had expressed on their death beds.

They fell into five themes. Things like 'I wish I hadn't worked so hard' or 'I wish I'd had the courage to live a life true to myself, not the life others expected of me'. I highly recommend her work.

It had a huge impact on me when I first came across it, so I'm a massive fan of Bronnie's, and therefore rather hesitant to suggest that, in my experience, there might actually be a sixth regret. I say this not from any experience in tending the dying (I have none), but from the thousands of emails I've received, and conversations I've had, over the years since *Fat, Forty and Fired* was published.

And what is this sixth regret? Well, judging from those emails and conversations, it is: 'I wish I'd had more sex.'

I'm not mentioning this sixth regret lightly or tritely. *They* weren't saying it lightly or tritely either. These were people in loving, long-term partnerships who bemoaned the fact that they had unwittingly ended up in sexless relationships.

There are a whole host of perfectly understandable reasons for people to no longer have a libido. Indeed, you don't need a reason – obviously, it's perfectly fine just not to have one. But for those who do wish they still felt sexual desire, it can be extremely distressing when they wake up and it is simply not there anymore.

The tales female readers have told me about the effects of menopause are harrowing. As are the accounts from male readers of erectile dysfunction and the like. It truly is a mine-field. I don't for one moment suggest sex is a simple issue, with one off-the-shelf answer for everyone. Every partnership is unique. Sex within them is a complex and sensitive area with a myriad of different approaches. All equally valid, as long as they work for the parties involved.

So, with all those caveats stated, what *am* I saying? Simply put, it's that *if you are in a long-term, committed, monogamous relationship, and you are no longer having sex and are not talking about that (or haven't talked about it), I can* guarantee *at least one of the partnership is unhappy about it.* Whatever they may claim in public. And by not addressing the issue honestly and kindly, big problems are building up that will have to be dealt with further down the track. That may be at a time when, unfortunately, it might be too late to undo the emotional damage that has been caused.

Of course, if you're in a relationship in which you've both discussed it, and happily agreed neither of you wants to have sex, that is fantastic. You've actually won the lottery in some ways – not having to negotiate the tricky issue of differing sex drives must be a blessing. So, I'm genuinely happy for those people and wouldn't suggest they should change a thing.

However, for people for whom sex has just fallen off the table and doesn't happen anymore, and who have never discussed the issue, I lovingly recommend that you don't kid yourself. Sweeping it under the carpet, and fooling yourself that she or he is as happy as you to be celibate, is more often than not a road to disaster. So, if you come to the point of deciding you don't want sex (again, which is absolutely fine and perfectly acceptable), what is your strategy if your partner hasn't?

Over the years, I've been told of hundreds of stories of how couples have managed a gap in their sex drives in their third trimester. The trouble is that it's so hard to know what to do, as even the best-intentioned approaches can cause unwitting pain.

'It's obvious he no longer finds me attractive, Nigel,' wrote one reader. 'He never makes a pass at me, and whenever I try something to make him interested, like wearing racy lingerie, I can tell he's embarrassed and simply goes through the motions to avoid hurting my feelings.'

Another reader told me how his wife ended up giving him an allotted sex session every Saturday afternoon at 4 pm.

'I appreciate the thought, but it's a disaster,' he told me. 'I don't want to be "let". I know she means well, but I find it so demeaning. Last week, she said to me, "You've got your ten minutes – do what you want with it." I don't simply want access to her body. I want us to have a joint, fun, intimate bonding experience together.'

Other approaches have been chillingly less empathetic.

'Oh *that*? Ugh. That's not my responsibility – he can take care of himself if he has to!' That's how one reader explained her view of the whole issue to me. Each to their own, but despite the wonders of masturbation I'd humbly suggest a little less contempt and a tad more understanding might be more beneficial in the situation.

More encouragingly, another reader told me, 'Our sex life is immeasurably better in our seventies than at any other time in our marriage. It was always hard to find the time during the busy years of career building and child rearing, but now that it's just the two of us at home, we've made it a priority and, though it might be hard to believe for a young 'un like you, it's rather unexpectedly wonderful – even if we aren't breaking any records, I'm sure.'

I suppose what it comes down to is that this issue needs to be spoken about, not ignored – however embarrassing or difficult the thought of doing so might be and in a kind, gentle and loving way. Just as happy, long-term couples talk about other issues in their relationship, why would we think it's a good idea that sex should be an exception and ignored? And, of course, the longer you don't discuss it, the harder it becomes to do so.

Importantly, even if discussing it might not result in you actually having more sex, just the acknowledgement of the existence of the topic is often enough. The rejected partner, who is having far less sex than they want, can end up feeling seen and heard, and, perish the thought, validated in their desire simply by the dialogue. And the partner who has little or no sex drive can be made to feel comfortable with that fact – not blamed or shamed.

As well, there are often game-changing, related benefits. As one female friend said to me, 'If it's about sex, it's not about the sex.'

'What on earth does that mean?'

'Well, issues in your sex life, particularly for women, are usually a consequence of *other* issues. Talking lovingly about the sex issue can be an excellent gateway to talk about the other real issues that might be far more important to address in your partnership.'

Another friend summed it up by saying, 'Sex should be the full stop in a relationship, not the full sentence.'

Yet another said, 'We made a decision early on in our marriage to always be "sexually generous" with each other. Never to avoid or weaponise it. Treat it lightheartedly and not let it become a source of misery. I know I shouldn't say this, but I suspect for some of my friends their lack of desire can actually be explained by a lack of imagination, choice and effort.'

This reminded me of the passage in A. A. Gill's autobiography where he writes about an early girlfriend who, when taking him to bed for the very first, and nervous, time, said to him reassuringly, 'Don't worry, we're going to do everything.'

It's not so much the 'everything' that I find lovely about it, but the use of the word 'we' and the playfully thoughtful attitude it conveys, in comparison with a 'you've got your ten minutes, do what you want with it' approach to proceedings.

But apart from any innate generosity you may or may not have on the topic, whichever way you look at it communication just seems a far better option than a third trimester full of unaddressed issues, rejection, guilt, secrets and resentment. Talking – and writing – about sex is a minefield in so many ways, but if it helps you get to lie on your deathbed and have none of the five regrets Bronnie mentions, or the sixth either, I feel it is well worth the effort.

54

The Tinder Train

FOR MANY OF us, getting to sixty involves having been with our partners for several decades, not merely years. That's a long time – and over that time, life happens. As I look around my friends of a similar age, the majority are not with their first husband or wife. Dear old 'straighty-180' Kate and Nigel are actually in the minority.

I mention this not out of any sense of superiority (as, Lord knows, although it is *very* much not my plan, we could be joining the majority in the blink of an eye), but because of the fascinating social group it has created. I'm not talking about the people who have re-partnered or remarried or happily committed to the single life. I'm talking about those in the process of looking for their next significant relationship.

And who find themselves on the Tinder Train in their fifties and sixties.

This is a very different experience than that of the twenty and thirty-year-olds on Tinder. We are talking an Entirely Different Experience.

I've had hundreds of conversations with both men and women on the unique form of torture that is online dating in your third trimester. It's one thing hopping into bed with a near stranger when you're slim, sexy and twenty, and another thing completely when you're slightly sad, saggy and sixty.

If you've spent thirty-odd years going to bed with the same person, it can be a shock to the system to get naked in front of someone new – and indeed see someone else other than your life partner get undressed before you.

'Jude and I had grown old together,' one man told me. 'We hadn't really noticed, or minded, the gradual deterioration in our physical state. We were comfortable with each other and our imperfections. We loved each other and had been happily walking around naked in each other's presence for years. But I tell you what, the first time I got naked with a woman I'd met online, it was a disaster.'

'How so?'

'We'd been out four or five times for dinner and got on like a house on fire. On this particular occasion, for the first time she invited me back to her place to stay the night. I was delighted to accept.

'Unfortunately, the moment we got naked, and I caught a glimpse of us in the mirror on her bedroom-cupboard door, I was so shocked at the state of us both that I immediately lost all desire. I knew it was illogical. And shallow. And hurtful.

But I simply couldn't go through with it – and I mean *really* couldn't go through with it.'

'You couldn't get an erection?'

'Well, I could. I mean I had. But after that moment, no. Hideous. Just hideous.'

My female friends also regale me with horror stories of disastrous dates with men in their third trimester. Many of these men are freshly out of long-term marriages and haven't been on a date in thirty years, so they don't have a clue how to converse with women.

'Honestly, he spent two and a half hours talking *at* me,' one woman explained to me. 'After sixty minutes of him talking about himself non-stop, I was beginning to despair of him ever asking me even one question – but eventually he did.

'He asked, "What do you think of US politics at the moment?" and without drawing breath, before I could answer, said, "Because if you ask me . . ."'

Another friend, who is about sixty, told me of the 'gender age tax'.

'This is the unwritten rule that men trade down in age when online dating. A sixty-year-old man expects to be going out with a woman in her mid-to-late forties. Or younger.'

'Meaning you're expected to go out with men in their seventies?' I asked.

'Precisely. Why I can't just date men my own age is beyond me, but apparently that's the way it is. Or the way they want it to be. It's as if they haven't noticed that their "market value" – shall we say – has declined slightly over the decades.

'I went out with one man, a photographer, who had clearly lied about his age on his profile, as well as using a totally misleading picture. He was a good twenty years older than me, but his demeanour was as if he was still a hot-shot photographer being chased by all the young models on his shoots, rather than the dowdy, overweight, unemployed grandfather I found out he now was. Of course, there's nothing wrong with being any of those things, but it's the pretence and the delusion that grates.'

Another told me how all the men she met were 'either after a nurse or a purse'. A memorable, chillingly depressing phrase.

Fortunately, amongst the horror stories, many end up finding love, despite having to kiss a few frogs along the way, so it's not all doom and gloom. It's fair to say, though, that the Tinder Train is a rite of passage I'd be happy to avoid in my third trimester if I possibly can.

55

The M word

I HAVE NO sisters, just one brother. I went to all-boys boarding schools throughout my education. My parents didn't have the sex chat with me. I never saw my mum naked. Periods were never mentioned. And not once in my entire home life did I see even one sanitary product.

Why am I telling you this? Because hopefully it goes some way to explaining my ignorance when it comes to menopause.

If you'd asked me, at, say, age twenty-five, what I knew about menopause, I'd probably have mumbled something about it being the month when an older woman's periods stop. But why would I know? No-one had ever told me anything about it, and why would I have gone and found out?

Nowadays, I wince when I look back at my youthful ignorance. My subsequent enlightenment won't reveal anything new to my female readers, but might be instructive for some of the male ones who share my poor early education.

For a start, it's not a month. Obviously. For many women it's a process that lasts years. In fact, for some, it's an ordeal that they will struggle with for the rest of their lives, never fully getting back on an even keel with their body or emotions.

As well, menopause isn't just when a woman's periods stop. If it was that simple, it might be something to look forward to and viewed as cause for celebration. But no – it is far more complex, the important impact of menopause being all the *other* stuff that stops and starts.

There is no one experience – everyone has a different story. In my conversations with women who have gone through it, the effects have included sleeplessness, weight gain, lack of libido, hot flushes, hair loss, wildly fluctuating emotions, brittle bones, impaired ability to concentrate, painfully inadequate secretions – vaginal, eyes and skin – bad acne and lack of energy. Truly a buffet of human misery. In Kate's case, less seriously and somewhat bizarrely, the symptoms also included her hair going straight after a lifetime of being wavy

And if the long list of potential effects isn't bad enough, it turns out I'm not the only one who doesn't properly understand it. When Kate went to the doctor to get help for her symptoms, she was offered anti-depressants. Now, granted, some women do suffer from depression brought on by menopause, but luckily Kate isn't one of them. Yet they were suggested to her all the same.

The Monty Python madness of going to the doctor for a list of ailments and being prescribed treatment for something else that you haven't got would be enough to make even the famous 'It's only a flesh wound' Black Knight give up.

But Kate struggled on. A year later, she went to another doctor – who also recommended anti-depressants. Luckily, she again held firm, eventually finding a doctor who prescribed her Hormone Replacement Therapy, which, in her case, is as near to a wonder drug as has ever been discovered. The point here isn't to suggest that HRT is the answer. In many cases, I'm sure anti-depressants are just the ticket. The point is that not only is menopause widely misunderstood, far too often it's mistreated as well.

So, again, why am I telling you this? Because for me there is an enormous opportunity here. If the men approaching their third trimester, who, like me, don't know squat about menopause, decided to educate themselves just a little bit, the overall sum of human happiness could be dramatically affected.

This isn't solely those with a female partner, because half the world is going to go through it. And if the other half is better educated about the issue, the appropriate empathy, understanding and support will be more readily available.

In my case, it simply was never on my radar until I was personally affected. But given it's an unavoidable part of the third trimester, it would seem to make sense to educate yourself (if you are indeed ignorant as I was) earlier than I did.

56

Pardon?

ONE HEALTH ISSUE that was on my radar was my hearing. A combination of swimming in the ocean and old age hasn't been kind to my ears. In *Fat, Forty and Fired* I wrote about the doctor telling me I was experiencing some auditory deterioration. So what had I done about it since? The square root of fuck all, that's what. A combination of denial, vanity and pigheadedness had kept me from taking action.

However, after one particularly bad weekend of constantly asking Kate to repeat herself and repeatedly being called an old deaf bastard in return, I was moved to book a test.

Talk about lamb to the slaughter. It was brutal. The lady conducting the test was delightful and professional – it was the exercises and results that were shocking.

For one exercise, I had to sit in a booth with headphones on whilst different sentences were played. After each one, my job was to repeat out loud what had just been said. As the exercise progressed, the background noise would steadily increase as the sentences themselves became slightly quieter.

For the first couple, there was no problem at all. 'The cat needs feeding,' I repeated, followed by 'The laundry is in the machine'.

The next couple weren't so easy. 'The school term starts soon?' I tentatively said, followed by 'Andrea is in hospital?'

The two after that, I simply motioned with my hands and a shrug that I couldn't even guess what was being said.

'How did I do?' I asked.

'Not so bad,' she kindly replied, 'I've seen worse.'

'So, no issue really?'

'It depends how you look at it.'

'Go on.'

'Well, you got the first two sentences correct.'

'Excellent.'

'Yes, but they were at the highest volume and clearest level. Your valiant guesses were incorrect on the second two *and there are eight other levels*. I'd hope a client would get at least seven of those correct.'

Yikes.

I ended up telling her of my frustrations at not being able to hear when Kate or the kids said something from another room. Of always having to shout, 'Hold on!' and walking nearer to ask them to repeat themselves. Of not being able to catch what was being said to me when there was any background noise. Of worrying that pretending to hear someone with a nod and a smile might be offensive, if I knew what they'd actually said.

Of choosing at social occasions not to speak to anyone but those directly next to me, because everyone else would be out of my range. Of the constant danger of guessing what had been said incorrectly and reacting inappropriately. Of pressing the phone painfully hard into my ear in an attempt to catch everything on a work call. Of making the knowingly limiting decision not to ask someone to repeat themselves twice, even if I couldn't hear them the second time. Of how, when I'm watching the rugby, my kids would walk into the room, complain about how loud it was and ask me to turn it down.

Long story short, I ended up agreeing to a two-week trial wearing hearing aids.

The results were astonishing. For the whole fortnight I didn't ask Kate to repeat herself once. My kids told me I was talking in a softer voice. I attended a function in a noisy restaurant and had conversations with people at both ends of the table many seats away from me. I caught everything on the phone. I heard things clearly that were said from other rooms. And on top of it all, no-one – not one person – noticed I was wearing them for the entire time. Whenever I confessed, people didn't believe me and I had to turn my head and bend my ear down to show them I wasn't making it up. The technology has come a very long way since the 'ear trumpet' days.

The real benefit of the trial, however, was realising how short-sighted – so to speak – my attitude towards my hearing loss had been, because the most damaging effects of poor hearing weren't the obvious things. It was the potentially devasting consequence of all the missed subtle clues.

For example, if I said to Kate, 'Sweetheart, could you take out the recycling?' and she were to reply, 'Sure, darling,' while underneath her breath muttering, '*Again*, you fuckwit?', but all I heard was 'Sure, darling', I would have missed the real communication.

But as my mate Becky says, 'Nigel, you need to be able to hear all the "You fuckwit"s, if you're to have a healthy relationship.'

The analogy I'd use is of reading glasses. I could easily get by without them. I'd simply hold menus at arms-length or ask one of my kids to read the small print for me. But it doesn't enter my head to merely 'get by'. Why would it? Instead, I wear reading glasses so I'm able to engage fully with the world without missing anything and constantly imposing on other people.

It's the same with my hearing. I can get by. Indeed, that is what I've been doing for the last twenty years. But at what cost? What have I been missing?

And how hypocritical is it for someone who wants to make the most of their third trimester to willingly accept not being able to hear properly and settle for getting by? I want to rip into the next decade, not be a passive, confused bystander throughout it.

The trouble is that the example of both my and Kate's parents wasn't exactly helpful. All of them experienced significant hearing loss and delayed taking effective action until it was absolutely imperative. And even then, my dear mum wouldn't turn them on for fear of running the battery down. Or, truth be told, because like so many old people, she'd left it too late to get onto the problem.

The contrast of hearing well was too stark and unsettling. The world seemed horribly noisy and jarring after years of muted sounds. 'I turned the kettle on, Nidgey, and almost had a heart attack. I had no idea it was so loud.'

I know a number of people whose hearing is as bad as, if not worse than, mine. A couple of them are, frankly, deaf as a post. And like I was, they are soldiering on without confronting the issue. And I get it. Confronting is the right word. I don't think of myself as a hearing-aid wearer either.

Glasses hint at learnedness and maturity. I'm embarrassed to admit that, on a business trip to America for a board meeting years ago, I bought and wore spectacles with entirely clear lenses. Ostensibly, I did it for a laugh. I wasn't going to tell anyone else they were clear, and therefore use that minor deception to help keep myself amused during the inevitably tedious proceedings. But, truth be told, I was secretly crapping myself about the heavy-hitting meeting and wanted to be taken more seriously during my presentation. Yeah, pretty lame, I know, but the funny thing is I think it actually worked and I *was* listened to a little more thoughtfully.

On the other hand, you'd be hard pushed to write a list of the benefits of showing off your hearing aids. You'd also have trouble finding aspirational role models who wear them. The singer Morrissey gave it a good go in the 1980s, occasionally wearing an ornamental hearing device, but still the clear societal clues remain that hearing aids shriek decrepitude. Therefore they're to be avoided if at all possible, and, if not, they're an embarrassing accessory best kept secret. They are also bloody expensive.

However, given I'm determined to be slightly smarter and a little less stupid in my sixties, after the trial I decided to bite the bullet and booked an appointment to invest in some hearing aids. But before I could follow through, events took an unexpected turn.

57

Queen Camel 6

DESPITE HER INCREASING poor health, the reliably frustrating way Mum answered the phone and my poor hearing, our daily calls were proving a success. It was worrying to get reports from my brother of the rapid progress of all her various ailments – even more so to hear her heavy breathlessness after the effort of just talking. But through it all she never failed, after reminding me of her phone number, to then make a point of saying how delighted she was I'd called, how she had been looking forward to it and, now that I had, that it had made her day. And she never ceased to sign off without telling me how much she loved me, Kate and the kids. It was wonderful to experience.

My parents were both fabulous people who did their very best for me, but Mum had rarely, if ever, previously expressed this type of emotional intimacy. Shown in action, yes; verbalised to the people concerned, no. For people of her generation and sensibilities, it just wasn't what you did. Well, she was now and I was loving it. I feel the previous year's trip had caused something of a breakthrough and taken our relationship to another level.

Now, we spent hours talking about and planning my next one, without dodging the elephant in the room that there might not be the opportunity for many more trips, given her precarious health; or as Mum put it, 'You better hurry up, Nidgey, else I can't guarantee I'll be above ground.'

Leaving family and work to travel to the UK from Australia is a big deal at the best of times, but during the Covid restrictions it was more than usually challenging. I had to time it right so I could get a number of commitments squared away (recording enough podcast episodes, finishing a couple of consultancy gigs, fitting in with Kate's schedule), so it wouldn't matter as much if I got stuck overseas and couldn't get back home for a while.

In conversations with Kate, colleagues and my brother, I finally decided to aim for a trip in late August. I called Mum to discuss this proposed timing with her. Something strange happened. Very strange.

When Mum picked up the phone, for the first time in my life she *didn't* say, 'Marston Magna 850172.'

Instead, she softly said, 'Can we not talk now, Nidgey?'

'Err, sure . . . of course, Mum. I'll call tomorrow?'

'That would be nice, dear.'

'Okay, love you.'

'Love you too, dear. Very much.'

And those were the last words she ever said to me. Barely six hours later, my brother called to say Mum had died.

She passed away sitting in her favourite chair in the conservatory at the back of the house, overlooking her beloved view of Corton Denham ridge. It was where she'd conduct her phone calls.

My brother and I spoke on FaceTime. He offered to show me her body and her face looked happier than I remember it being for months. Logically I was pleased she wouldn't have to suffer anymore. Emotionally I was a mess, though, and grief came in unexpected waves. I knew it wasn't a tragedy or unexpected – she was eighty-seven and riddled with cancer, for Christ's sake – but it was still a shock. And it made me so sad I'd not got out there again to see her one last time. I was all the more grateful I'd spent that precious month with her the year before. Such important memories.

It felt different to when my dear dad died. He had been suffering from dementia for a number of years, so we'd become heartbreakingly used to him 'not being there' before his actual death. And when he passed we still had one parent left. Now I was officially orphaned.

For the last twenty years, since we'd moved to Australia I would think on a weekly basis, 'Oh, I must tell Mum or Dad that.' I'd regularly snap pictures on my phone of one or other of the kids doing something and send it to them at random. Or email a silly message.

The very morning of the 'Can we not talk now, Nidgey' call, I'd sent Mum pictures of Grace in Canberra. In the days following her death, I caught myself having the same thoughts, then realising that Granny wasn't there to see the picture of Eve and Mattie that I was in the process of sending her.

Mothers are so often the glue that binds broader family members together and I found myself sadly wondering if her death meant the Australian Marshes and UK Marshes would slowly, but inevitably, slip further and further apart. So many thoughts.

One of the rituals I'd invented in my campaign to build up a meaningful connection with her in recent years was 'The Daily Flower'. I'd brought a small vase from the Queen Camel pottery home to Sydney and tried to remember every day to pick a flower for it and send a photo of it to Mum. Now, it cruelly served the opposite purpose. With or without a flower, it was a reminder that she was gone.

It was difficult to know how to respond when friends who didn't know the news greeted me with the traditional Aussie 'How you going?' Did I pretend and respond with my usual 'Never been better' or did I tell them? Either choice had its obvious downsides – lie or burden someone with awkward information to deal with.

One choice that wasn't hard, however, was the one between virtually attending the funeral and being there in person. I had no doubt I was going to be there, whatever it took.

58

Alphabet dinners

ONE OF THE surprising upsides of the whole Covid malarkey for me has been the establishing of our alphabet dinners. It's a tradition I now hold in as much affection as the longstanding Marsh Messenger group.

The idea came about after weeks and weeks of lockdown, as an attempt to brighten the monotony and look after each other's mental health. Basically, we started a weekly ritual whereby every Saturday we had a family dinner built on a letter theme. The letter was chosen at random the week before – for example, 'V'. Then each person who was attending had to contribute a 'V' dish. From scratch; not buy it premade or order in.

Everything had to be 'V' themed – starter, main course, dessert, drinks – the whole lot. So on the 'V' night, for instance, I made vol-au-vents, the drink was a vodka cocktail, the main course vermicelli noodles, dessert vanilla cheese cake. You get the idea.

It was surprisingly good fun. Especially for someone like myself who is no great shakes in the kitchen. It gave me a reason to experiment and a supportive occasion to mess up as I did. Wonderfully, it also created within the family a sense of anticipation and communication throughout the week, shared endeavour during the preparation process on the day, raucous hilarity over the meal itself, and endless stories to be retold long after it was over.

The tradition evolved and was tweaked as the weeks went by. For the 'U' dinner, a national theme was adopted. Harry made Uruguayan flat bread, Eve Ukrainian stone cake and I adapted a drinking ritual from Uzbekistan.

Throughout the evening there were to be six rounds of non-alcoholic shots of different flavours (lime, chocolate, chilli etc) I had prepared ready to go. Each person was assigned a round between a course. When it was their turn, they had to stand up, draw the name of one of the other diners out of a hat, say something nice about that person, then shout '*Yaks shi sog'lik!*' (Uzbek for 'Good health!'), raise their glass, and, with the rest of the group, down the shot in one and place the empty shot glass upside down on the top of their head.

It was ridiculous – but poignant – hearing siblings saying touchingly nice things about each other. And hilarious when we all spluttered through the chilli shot – the hottest chillies, with the seeds left in, having been mischievously used.

For the 'T' dinner I compiled a twenty timeless tunes playlist to accompany the rather eclectic, but delicious never-theless, meal of Turkish bread and tzatziki, tuna sashimi, tom yum soup and tapioca pudding. It's fair to say that, on the night, the kids took issue with my definition of 'timeless', but I still had heaps of fun reliving my youth, putting together a list of songs from 'T artists' such as The The, Talk Talk, Thompson Twins and the Tom Tom Club.

Whatever the letter, there always seemed to be a way for everyone to join in and different angles to take. We live in trepidation of the online random letter chooser picking 'Z' one day, but I feel we'll find a way to rise to the occasion if it does.

Reflecting on the dinners, I realise there's a lesson to be learned – beyond the fact that vol-au-vents are a bit shit if you overcook the pastry. The dinners are so much fun and so freeing, precisely *because they are so rule based and restrictive.*

The Russian composer Stravinsky famously said, 'Give me the freedom of a tight brief,' believing that if the structure were non-negotiable it would both free him up to concentrate on the quality of the composition – rather than the format – and force him to be creative with it. It's part of the reason I am so passionate about the strict Five of My Life format.

In life, we often need something to push off, fight against. All those years as a child complaining about, and finding, ways around school uniform rules might actually have been good for you. You think things would be better, and kids would be happier, if we did away with all those silly rules about skirt lengths and ties. But would they? I'm not so sure.

There's an African proverb about how no-one likes being chased up a tree by a lion, but they always enjoy the view when they get to the top. My father and I used to argue about his, to my eyes, ridiculous commitment to 'standards'. Make your bed, comb your hair, brush your shoes, write letters properly, etc.

Now, I think I understand better what he was getting at. After decades of hating being told what to do and railing against stupid rules, I realise that being forced to do stuff and follow rituals – however arbitrary – isn't always such a bad thing. You could, after all, play tennis without a net, but it wouldn't really be tennis, would it? We could have decided it was a bit difficult coming up with a fourth course for our 'U' dinner, and not bother, but the udon soup produced after a bit of extra thought was definitely worth the effort.

However, delicious though the Japanese soup might have been, there are always some rules that are so moronic that they *demand* to be fought against.

59

Zoom

GETTING TO MUM's funeral was going to be easier said than done. It was the height of the Covid crisis in Australia and the government was imposing severe travel restrictions in a bid to deal with the pandemic.

Part of this was that you had to apply to the federal government for a travel exemption to be allowed to leave the country. Even if you were granted one, there was no guarantee you could get back into Australia when you wanted, as the return process was equally challenging. And when you eventually managed to re-enter the country, it involved a costly two weeks' quarantine locked in a hotel room.

As well, the airlines had slashed the number of flights and more than doubled the cost of international tickets in a bid to stave off bankruptcy. And even if you could get the money together for the trip, find the time off from home commitments and be granted a travel exemption, you still had to pass a Covid test seventy-two hours prior to departure. If that proved positive the whole thing was off, anyway. Lastly, I'd have to find flights on an airline that transited in a 'Green Zone' – as determined by the British government – otherwise I'd have to quarantine for two weeks upon arrival in the UK, thereby missing the funeral.

The majority of people I spoke to advised me not to attempt the trip. To stay at home, look after the living, and honour the dead by attending the funeral on Zoom. I'm making no judgement on the choices that others have made, but I simply couldn't get my head around not doing *everything* in my power to attend in person.

On one level, I realised it didn't matter, but on another deeply personal level it mattered to me very much indeed. I knew I'd regret it to my own dying day if I didn't at least make every effort to be there. So I stuck to my resolve and set about trying to get a flight, exemption and negative test in time.

The flight proved surprisingly easy – if expensive. And risky. Kate found an economy ticket, at almost four times the normal price, via Singapore that would get me there just in time. They were selling fast, so I immediately bought it, even before getting a travel exemption. I wanted to secure the seat, because by the time I applied and received an answer from the government, it was clear there'd be no flights left, even if I was granted permission to fly.

Next, I applied to the government for a travel exemption. These were like hen's teeth, but on the form there was a category for consideration entitled 'compassionate grounds'.

I filled it out, explaining the situation, and sent it off the same night. Barely four hours since I'd learnt of Mum's death and two positive steps already taken. I was quietly hopeful.

Not for long.

An email in my inbox the next day from the Australian Department of Home Affairs informed me:

I have considered your request and as an authorized decision maker determined that this travel is not exempt from the travel restrictions.

Margaret

The irony of the fact that the bearer of the bad news shared my mum's name wasn't lost on me. Nor the casually disrespectful lack of a last name in the email sign-off. I'm not saying Margaret was a small-minded bureaucrat drunk on a cruel power trip, but it did cross my mind that maybe Covid had provided her with the very first opportunity in her miserable existence to be 'an authorized decision maker'.

The newspapers were full of stories of Hollywood stars, politicians and wealthy business leaders flying in and out of the country with joyful abandon, so the death of my last remaining parent not qualifying as adequate compassionate grounds seemed ridiculous. Why have the bloody section on the form if you were never going to grant it? And just what *would* qualify as compassionate grounds if the death of a parent didn't?

I remembered the heartless jobsworths at the insurance company who had gleefully put bureaucracy before humanity after my dad's death. That time, I didn't have the will to fight and simply let them steal my money so I could focus on the grieving process instead. This time I didn't want the idiots to win. And besides, I had to fight if I were to have any chance of getting to the funeral.

After multiple emails and calls, the lack of a death certificate was finally established as the remaining reason being clung to in defence of the rejection. I had been twice vaccinated, I had somewhere to stay in UK for months if need be. I was both an Australian and British citizen. And, importantly, there was no possible way I was a Covid risk to Australia, as I was asking to *leave* the country, not enter it.

The sticking point was a form. A bureaucratic form. Not for the first time, I was reminded of the sad maxim that systems are inhumane, humans are kind. For the world to be set on the right course, the latter has to take precedence over the former.

It makes me angry writing about it so I will cut a long story short. We managed to get them a death certificate. And systems being systems, they then immediately approved my application.

I passed my Covid test, flew to Singapore, then on to London. As the flight touched down at Heathrow, I was struck by the slightly bizarre realisation that, twenty years ago, I had missed my twin daughters' first birthdays because I was on a plane from the UK to Australia, and here I was now, missing their twenty-first birthdays because I was on a flight the other way.

I made a mental note to make it up to them on my return, as I walked through customs to be met by my brother for the drive to the West Country for the funeral the next morning.

60

The Queen is dead

I STAYED ALONE in Mum's house the night before the funeral. It was exactly how I'd remembered it from my last visit. But the simple fact that Mum was dead made the house seem soulless, smaller – shabby, even. I was surprised and ashamed to think this. Previously it had never appeared anything other than a perfectly normal loving home. Now it brought to mind Philip Larkin's 'Home Is Sad' poem – without anyone to please, 'it withers so . . .'

Jetlag prevented me from being able to sleep so I went searching for something to read. Mum had been a voracious reader and her many shelves were crammed end-to-end with neatly displayed books. I noticed that one, however, was on its side. It was placed as if in the process of being read.

I picked it up to see it was my '50 book'. It had a dedication to her above a picture of us both in a café in Sydney, taken on one of her visits to Australia. I opened it to read the inscription I'd handwritten inside: 'Mum, you are a wonderful mother, grandmother, and friend. Kate and the kids love you very much. As do I.' I swallowed back a gulp. Flicking through the book, I noticed she had placed little yellow sticky notes on every page that I had written about her.

The next morning, I opened the curtains to what was obviously going to be the perfect day, weather wise. And, it turned out, every other wise as well.

I will forever be grateful that I was there in person. It couldn't have been a more fitting, respectful and appropriately sad day. There was even cause, on occasion, for private amusement.

Before I'd got inside the church I was approached by a variety of Mum's friends from the village, who told me how much she'd loved my twice daily calls – at the start of each day to wish her good morning and at the end to say goodnight.

Twice daily? I'd never called her twice in the same day in my life.

I couldn't help but chuckle to myself, remembering Mum's habit of embellishing the truth to improve her yarns. It's a habit I've inherited, as I can't see why the facts should be allowed to get in the way of a good story – as long as it remains true in spirit. I had, after all, called *regularly*. Given the church setting, it reminded me of my university religious studies and the reaction of some of my more naïve fellow students upon being told that 'forty days and forty nights' didn't literally mean that, but simply a long time. If it's good enough for Mum and the Bible, I'm fine with it.

The sadness even had its upsides. After my reading at the start of the service, I was unexpectedly – and to my horror – tearful. Hard as I tried, I simply couldn't stop the waterworks. As I sat back down in the pew, I felt my brother take my hand, squeeze it gently, and hold it for the entire time until he had to get up to give the eulogy. It was an exquisite moment of brotherly love that I'll never forget.

He gave a sensational address, capturing the essence of our mother perfectly. The vicar then knocked it out of the park with a speech that managed to be both passionate and sincere, without being hectoring. Reminding the congregation that to love is to be vulnerable, and that being heartbroken is both inevitable and a sign that you loved and were loved.

And on top of it all, the village church provided a sublime setting for proceedings. It evoked a mysterious innate sense that we were somewhere important and appropriate for the particular occasion. A setting where you could feel the breeze of history.

For over seven hundred years, people like me have come to sit within these walls to honour their dead – seeking solace, reassurance and meaning. Walls that in English writer John Ruskin's words have been 'washed by passing waves of humanity'. You feel a mutuality with the rest of mankind, both through the centuries and around the world. A sense of the essence of society and what it is to be human.

And these feelings are not something I would have got from a bloody Zoom call, if I'd let Margaret from the Australian Department of Home Affairs thwart my travel plans.

Rituals matter. Ceremonies matter. They're an important part of what separates us from other animals. We could choose to throw our dead in the rubbish tip, rather than bury them according to tradition. But, of course, we *just know* that would be wrong.

I understand that millions of people had no choice during the pandemic other than to attend funerals of loved ones on Zoom. I feel enormous sympathy (anger in many cases), although I'm pleased that Zoom at least enabled some form of connection and attendance.

I feel there's a real danger of dehumanisation here if we don't go back to how it was. On Zoom you are *watching* the funeral, but you aren't *part* of it. You aren't holding your brother's hand, or being told of your mother's hilarious embellishments by her friends in the village, or throwing dirt on the coffin. Some things in life, and death, are worthy of enormous effort, risk and inconvenience. And should substantially disrupt our normal life and thought patterns.

Here endeth the lesson.

61

Queen Camel 7

WITH THE FUNERAL over, the focus shifted to the not inconsiderable task of clearing Mum's house. I say 'not inconsiderable', because, although her home was of a modest size, not only was every surface covered with knick-knacks and every wall plastered with photos, every single cupboard, shelf and drawer was stuffed to overflowing. She clearly had never thrown anything away.

Those novelty table napkins from our time living in America in the 1970s? Yep, folded, ironed and put away for the last fifty-five years behind the spare blankets in the guest bedroom. *Worried that the eighteen wooden spoons in the various kitchen drawers might not be enough?* Don't be, as I've just found another sixty in two flower pots on top of the cupboard in the laundry room.

In Dad's study I found a shoebox with 'NIGEL'S TREASURES' written on the lid in Mum's famously appalling handwriting. Nigel's treasures? What could they be? It turns out that they were six small toys from a variety of stages of my early childhood, all clearly labelled.

There was a fluffy sheep Dad had brought back from Iceland. A metallic donkey from a family holiday in Ireland, which still walked and hee-hawed when you turned the key in its side. Also, a small wooden dog that I remembered from the photo of me holding it as a four-year-old that had been stuck on Mum's kitchen wall for decades. I'm not sure I'd describe it as a treasure, but I couldn't resist putting the dog in my pocket (I'm looking at it now in its new home, on my desk, as I write).

The enormity of the task was made slightly easier by the valuation my brother had organised earlier. A professional had gone through the house to officially value its contents, so he could give a report to the solicitor in charge of carrying out Mum's will. As part of this probate process, he was legally bound to list all the individual items deemed to be worth more than 250 pounds (about 450 dollars).

'Guess how many of Mum's belongings are worth more than 250 pounds,' my brother asked me.

'Oh mate, I haven't a clue,' I replied.

'Just take a wild punt.'

'Err, okay – 100?'

'Lower.'

'Eighty?'

'Lower.'

'Fucking hell, mate, just tell me already!'

'None.'

'None?'

'None.'

Okay, so at least during the clearing-out process we didn't need to worry that we might inadvertently recycle something worth a fortune.

I did, however, learn something surprising from his valuation report. He had to put items into four categories. Apart from those worth more than 250 pounds, he also identified those that might have some residual collective value at auction (seventy-eight wooden spoons, anyone?), mark those that were worthless and . . . inform us of those items that were 'less than worthless'.

How the fuck in our Lord's name could something be 'less than worthless'? My brother explained that there were certain things we legally weren't permitted to give to charity shops, take to the council recycling centre or even throw out – because they were deemed dangerous.

This included Mum's sofa and armchairs. Apparently, they weren't fire retardant and the stuffing was suspected to be made out of something slightly worse than asbestos. My brother said we might have to pay to get them taken away. And there was I, thinking 'couldn't give it away' was just a figure of speech.

Along with these possessions were boxes and boxes of papers Mum had collected and carefully kept throughout her life. They contained countless things that had no meaning in our eyes – such as her grandmother's pony-riding certificates and electrician bills for servicing the boiler from the 1950s.

However, there were others that were fascinating. Like the government leaflet from 1940 entitled 'If The Invader Comes – What To Do, And How To Do It'. The leaflet detailed the six-point plan UK civilians were to follow if the Germans made it across the Channel, how to avoid being 'machine gunned from the air', and how citizens should be extra cautious to check 'a military officer is really British, not a German pretending to be so'. It's amazing to think that was her reality as an eight-year-old girl. A different world.

There was also the pamphlet she'd received upon announcing her engagement, which gave tips on how to 'be a good wife', such as: 'Dispute not with him, be the occasion what it may: but much rather deny yourself the trifling satisfaction of having your own will'. A different world indeed.

There were also letters. So many, many letters. It was impossible to go through all of them, as it would have taken months. Instead, we dipped into one or two in every box in an attempt to get an idea of the contents and a view into the past.

On the second day of sorting through these boxes, I spotted a letter from Scotland to Belgium. We used to live in Brussels and Mum's only sibling, Daisy, had lived in Glasgow, so I picked it up to peruse. I took out the four handwritten pages, but before beginning to read I flipped to the back page to check it was, indeed, from Daisy. There at the bottom of the last page was her signature; however, underneath was a slightly non-traditional sign-off.

Her sister hadn't concluded with 'Lots of love' or 'Talk soon' or 'Love you, sis'. No, instead she had written in big capital letters, and underlined it twice: 'I HATE YOUR GUTS.'

62

Lettergate

STUNNED, I READ the letter from my aunt to Mum out loud to my brother. Four pages of passionate grievances, accusations and anger. We didn't know what to say, so instead decided to read the rest of the letters in the box – and discovered many more in the same vein.

There had obviously been the most appalling rift between sisters dragging on for years. And it was one that was never resolved – sadly, Daisy had passed away before they had the chance to. The disputes were wide ranging but most centred around their mum – Nana, as my brother and I had called her. There were letters from every party concerned: Daisy, Mum, Nana, Nana's second husband. All served to reveal a complex tale over the years of relationship misery.

I've spent a lot of time thinking about these letters. And in a bid to find a silver lining, I've come to a number of conclusions in my quest to be slightly smarter and a little less stupid in my third trimester.

The first is that I have absolutely no desire to become a student of the rift to discover what caused it, to take sides or apportion blame. I genuinely couldn't care less. No, that's not quite true – it's stronger than that; I positively don't want to find out.

There are always three sides to every story – his, hers and the truth. And in this case trying to establish the truth would be entirely wasted energy. Moreover, if you could uncover the truth – so what? How would that serve Mum or Aunty Daisy, as they're both long dead. Or me? Or anyone?

One of Kate's mother's favourite films is *What We Did on Holiday*. I watched it with her the week after the funeral. It's a funny movie, but in the closing scene there is also a serious message. In it, one of the lead characters makes a speech at a funeral where he says, 'The truth is, every human being on the planet is ridiculous in their own way. So we shouldn't judge, we shouldn't fight. Because in the end . . . in the end, none of it matters.'

I thought back to the notice in the newspaper announcing Mum's death: eight lines on page twenty-six. It was entirely dwarfed by the other news on the same page, let alone on all the other pages. It served as a reminder that even an entire life of a loved one is insignificant compared to a single day's news, and therefore an individual grievance of that person is a speck of sand, when compared to the infinite canopy of human existence and activity.

Bearing this in mind, and borrowing an expression from my daughters, I decided that the ins and outs of my own family's historical split deserved no more than a rueful shrug and a 'whatev'.

My second observation was how pleased I was that the rift hadn't leaked into the next generation. Both my brother and I had always got on wonderfully with our cousins in Scotland. Indeed, Kate and I had been in the process of planning a trip to see them all when Covid had closed down international travel.

Intergenerational trauma so often comes with these types of issues. Grudges might be held on behalf of others and attempts made to rectify perceived grievances for people who wouldn't benefit, or even realise, if they were rectified as *they were already under ground*. It's a type of madness and one I've no desire to indulge.

Call me naïve, but the third conclusion surprised me. In chatting about it with friends it soon transpired that this type of familial warfare was common. Alarmingly common. Every person I raised it with seemed to have their own version of family in-fighting. Close relations perpetually at each other's throats, years remorselessly and joylessly spent trying to prove one point or the other.

Brothers spitefully competing so one of them could be seen 'to win'. Bitterly contested wills. Sisters viciously vying for a greater share of a mother's attention and approval. A daughter refusing to talk to her father for decades. Parents declining to attend the wedding and even the funeral of one of their sons.

I found the stories of parents estranged from their children the most upsetting, and hearing all of these tales of woe in a short space of time was extremely sobering. What on earth is wrong with us as a species?

In the latter cases, the root cause was perceived injustices visited upon children by their parents. I shudder to think of the multitude of things I've said and done that I'd do differently if I had my time again. I believe that in the main people try their best, but as a parent of four myself, '*What trauma might I have created for my own kids*' was the lens through which I listened with rapt horror to these stories.

Four common categories quickly became evident. The first was injustices that seemed (to someone not involved at the time) so insignificant: 'I always got hand-me-down clothes, never new ones'; 'I had to share a bedroom with my brother, while my sister had her own room'. The second was what I'd call imagined grievances: 'Mum clearly preferred my younger sister'; 'My parents didn't approve of my career choice/partner/ sexuality'. When asked to provide evidence for such claims, the proof might be flimsy at best and self-servingly delusional at worst. It became obvious that different children could, and did, hear exactly the same parental conversations and retain wildly contrasting conclusions from them.

The third category was collateral damage from hardwired, historical, casual sexism. It was something I know that my Aunty Daisy had to deal with. Our family folklore was full of tales of her presenting her mum with something seriously impressive she'd done as a young child, like build a fully functioning space rocket, only to be pushed aside with an enthusiastic yelp of 'Oh, never mind *that* – look! John next door has done a finger painting'.

We used to laugh at the retelling of these stories, thinking no harm had been done. More fool us, obviously. Kate's own aunt had had an eerily similar experience with her parents, recounting how when she and her brother went home he was always given a drink and asked questions about his fascinating training in the RAF, while she'd be whisked into the kitchen to help prepare the dinner – the fact that she was three years older and training to be a doctor casually ignored.

Sadly, the third category was those cases where real, awful injustice and cruelty had been visited upon children by one or both of their parents. These were terrible, heartbreaking stories.

Yet a strange inverse pattern was present. In the minor cases, grievances (real or perceived) tended to be ferociously clung to like life rafts. And not only clung to, but nurtured and polished to become a central victim narrative that coloured their entire existence.

This contrasted starkly with many of the appalling cases I was told where the genuine awful injustice had been let go. Astonishingly, case in point, a guest on 5ML, Dr Gregory Smith, whose childhood had included some horrendous treatment, telling me he not only forgave his father, but loved him as well.

This brings me on to my fourth observation. These rifts are such needless, wasted and *avoidable* effort. They might make for an excellently entertaining TV series (how good is *Succession*?!), but in the real world it does seem to me to be the absolute pinnacle of 'missing the point' to spend one's life battling those closest to you.

I understand there are families where simply appalling things have happened that can't be forgotten. However, I'm talking here about those lives where people choose – consciously or subconsciously – to make and nurture a drama. Out of molehills. They repeatedly ignore the fog horn of love sounding off right next to them and focus instead on the faint whisper of a slight from a hundred metres – or years – away.

I'm not suggesting that people should aim to be best – or even good – friends with every one of their family members.

That would be setting yourself up for failure. What I'm talking about is proactively deciding in advance to refuse to allow a schism between yourself and any close blood relative. Ever. Without exception. I believe it's achievable if the task is approached with genuine love in your heart.

This leads to my fifth and final takeout from 'Lettergate'. Namely that I'm determined, in my third trimester, to do all in my power to never cause, enable or contribute to that situation in my own family.

Importantly, this starts with proper acknowledgement of how flawed, incredibly annoying and mind-bendingly wrong I can be. There is a reason I chose the second word in this book's title. I'm painfully aware that you can't please all the people all the time, and how, unwittingly, I might often press all the wrong buttons with certain people. And I'm committed to being non-defensively open to feedback and working on my flaws.

At the same time, I'm equally committed to never amplifying or inflaming any family issues. Instead, trying to calm things down and to see things from the other's point of view and in their proper, broader context (will this matter in ten minutes, ten months, ten years?). And I'll try to force myself to 'let it go' whenever I feel myself being dragged into ungenerous thoughts about those we're supposed to love the most.

Of course, I'm not advocating being a doormat. However, I am suggesting treating each of your family members as an exception that gets special treatment. So often we reserve the worst of ourselves for those closest to us. Try to reverse that dynamic. Give *them* – not your work colleagues or book-club buddies – the best of yourself. Have special higher standards of tolerance and behaviour where they're concerned.

View it as a game, if you must – one where you get points for never taking offence. Double points if you help another family member avoid negative thoughts and destructive words or actions themselves. Be a fountain, not a drain. This is particularly important if you're in your third trimester. *Time is running out.*

Mend those bridges now, rather than be standing at a graveside full of regret, wondering what on earth all the fuss was about and dearly wishing you'd told someone you loved them really – despite all the squabbles over stupid issues that when faced with the finality of death, seem all the more trivial and moronic.

And if all else fails, and the above is too much for you, at the very least make a point of always, always, thinking twice before posting that letter.

63

Mattie

When I returned to Australia after Mum's funeral, it was clear all was not well with our dog, Mattie. She was getting old. A hundred and twelve, in fact, if I've got my human to dog years conversion correct. In anyone's language, it's a good innings – but one suggesting not too long a future ahead.

I was surprised at how much this thought upset me. I've never been a dog person. As a child we had cats. Truth be told, my feeling towards dogs always used to be one of either fear or irritation.

We'd got Mattie for the kids. I was happy to sign up for the responsibility, and cost, for their sakes, but didn't intend or expect to develop any real feelings for her. She started life sleeping out of sight in a mango box on an old jumper at the foot of the washing machine, and over the years gradually worked her way out of the laundry, and fruit basket, and up the stairs into a proper dog basket at the foot of our bed. And into my heart.

She was just so cute. And loyal. And reliable. And positive. I actually think she helped make me a better man.

I used to resent having to take her for a walk and the cost of her upkeep. Now whilst I joked about the buggerance of needing to carry her up and down the stairs that she could no longer manage, I secretly enjoyed and looked forward to it. And in worrying signs of my softening heart, I'd recently bought a dog cookbook for my daughter so she could make Mattie some more enjoyable meals, as I felt guilty about the boring dry kibble we'd been feeding her all her life.

Despite my initial standoffishness, and all that dry kibble, she loved us wholeheartedly, without judgement, for sixteen years. Always pleased to see any of us. Always expectantly at the front door when we returned home. Always choosing to move to lie in whichever room we were in. She was now half-blind, three-quarters deaf, 100 per cent suffering from Cushing disease, and was crippled with arthritis in her back legs. Yet she still managed a tail wag and smile whenever we called her name – eager to get up and limp to whichever one of us had called, in the hope of an ear scratch, tummy tickle or maybe – joy of joys – a chicken liver treat.

Back when I was a young non-pet-owning executive in an ad agency, I'd worked on a dog-food account and remember scoffing to myself when we were taken through the research saying that pet owners loved their dogs as *genuine members of their families.* I wince at the ignorance of my youth – as now, approaching sixty, that is *exactly* how I, and we, viewed Mattie. A family member I was dreading saying goodbye to. And the kids having to live without.

They'd literally grown up with her. For years she had been the first person they said hello to when they came back from school, the last person they said goodnight to when they went to bed, and the first person they said good morning to when they woke up. They set up an Instagram page for her – rather unflatteringly, but unarguably accurately, called Mattie The Fattie – that never failed to brighten my day whenever I scrolled through it.

So it was achingly sad when her decline had become so advanced that it was becoming cruel to keep her alive any longer. Along with all her other ailments, she now could no longer stand, let alone walk to her water bowl, so on our vet's advice we arranged for a visit from their recommended expert who dealt with these matters.

The rather appropriately named Dr Raphael Dye was excellent at his job. Softly spoken, calm and patient, he made what was a naturally tearful and upsetting occasion go as well as possible in the circumstances. All the family was there, and as we gathered around the grave I had dug in the back garden I couldn't help thinking this was truly the end of an era. Mum gone, dog dead, house empty. For twenty-odd years our home had been noisily and messily full of six humans and a dog. Any overnight visitor had had to make do with a doona on the sofa, as there was no such thing as a guest room. Now in the space of two short months the house had emptied.

With all the kids moved out and Mattie no longer with us, it would be just me and Kate in The Burrow as we entered our third trimester together. At least we'll have a spare bed to offer as we do.

Conclusion

As I WRITE this, I'm in the middle of thinking about planning a weekend away to celebrate our thirtieth wedding anniversary. If that doesn't make me feel old, I don't know what will. And as with *Fat, Forty and Fired* and *Fit, Fifty and Fired Up*, I'm publishing it eighteen months or so before the actual decade in question. Prompting Kate to remark, 'It's just like you to finish early, Nigel.' I've no idea what she meant by that.

So how to wrap it all up? Well, despite all the inevitable shite that I, and Kate, will have to deal with as our bodies and careers fall apart, I am genuinely looking forward to my next decade with something nearing puppy-dog enthusiasm. However, rather than tempt fate by going on about how lucky I feel, I thought instead I'd give an update as to where I've got to with some of the issues I've raised in the preceding chapters.

Drink? Still sober, despite the errant bottle of Holsten.

Hearing aids? I followed through and am now keenly aware of just how many 'You fuckwit's I have been missing.

Relationship status? Still married, hopefully – otherwise, I'm going to look bloody stupid on that weekend away.

Weight? Surprisingly and satisfyingly, it is indeed at its ideal level. We'll see how long that lasts.

The Five of My Life? I was fortunate to find new business partners in DM Media (the lovely people who gave the Podcast of the Year award back at the start), so I intend to keep doing 5ML for as long as the dear Lord allows.

Children? All off doing their own things in locations from Canada to Canberra and all points in between. And not remotely children anymore.

The Burrow? Unusually quiet and clean, but reassuringly some things never change as it persists in both leaking *and* flooding whenever Sydney turns on one of its downpours.

Messenger? The family group chat continues to be a daily source of pleasure. The names have changed yet again, so although I'm can't be entirely sure which of my family members is 'faf de klerk', 'frontline material' or 'volvon', I love the regular banter nevertheless.

Career? I suspect I'm unemployable in a conventional job, but I do continue to get hired to do speaking and consultancy gigs. And rather unexpectedly a new line of coaching work has started to take off (maybe the one career positive of being – and looking – old is that it suggests wisdom . . .)

US film and TV progress? I'll get back to you later – oh, look, there's Halley's Comet.

Deep-sea diving? Never done any, despite my Google profile continuing to claim – in the face of repeated efforts to correct it – that this is how I make my living.

Drawing? I try to put pencil to paper at least once a day and I like to think I'm slowly getting marginally more proficient.

Bronte Biathlon? I believe I've held on to the dubious distinction of most races ever lost by one member. On the flipside, it's possible I also hold the record for the most bits of litter picked up on the walk to the start line.

The brown dot that my dentist didn't like the look of? Mercifully, for now, benign.

Self-help books? I remain conflicted.

Queen Camel? Mum's house has long been sold, but the family's connection to the village remains, as the church grave-yard will always be her and Dad's final resting place and forever in my thoughts.

Thank you for reading. I wish each and every one of you love, happiness and laughter – whatever trimester you may be in.

Acknowledgements

THANKS TO TARA Wynne, Caitlan Cooper-Trent and all the wonderful team at Curtis Brown.

Thanks as well to Sophie Ambrose, Patrick Mangan, Adam Laszczuk, Veronica Eze, Laura Nimmo and Michael Epis. I feel blessed to work with, and be published by, Penguin Random House.

To all the readers who have sent me messages of encouragement over the years since *Fat, Forty and Fired*, thank you. They meant, and mean, the world to me.

And Kate. This book would be a mess without you. As would I.

Discover a
new favourite

Visit **penguin.com.au/readmore**